COLD

THE UNSOLVED MURDERS OF SEVEN YOUNG WOMEN

KEVIN DAMASK

CKBooks Publishing

Contact Kevin Damask at kevindamask.substack.com.

ISBN: 978-1-949085-90-7 (paperback)
978-1-949085-91-4 (ebook)

Cover photo by Kevin Damask

CKBooks Publishing
PO Box 214
New Glarus, WI, 53574
ckbookspublishing.com

This book is dedicated to the family and friends of Christine Rothschild, Debra Bennett, Julie Speerschneider, Julie Hall, Susan LeMahieu, Shirley Stewart and Donna Mraz.
May the cherished memories you made with them live on forever in your hearts.

TABLE OF CONTENTS

Introduction

Retired journalist George Hesselberg, a former reporter and columnist at the *Wisconsin State Journal*, provided valuable advice as I was starting to work on this project: Journalists don't try to solve crimes; they try to better understand them.

That was my primary goal as I spent the past couple of years researching, interviewing sources and writing about seven cold case mysteries that occurred in Madison, Wisconsin. What happened to seven young women, all around the same age, between 1968-1982? Why haven't the cases been solved? Was a serial killer running around southern Wisconsin in the late '70s and early '80s? And why was key evidence destroyed by local law enforcement? Evidence that likely contained DNA and a possible link to the killer.

When I started working on this project in 2020, I was poised to write a book about Wisconsin's most notorious cold case murders. However, the more I dug into it, I realized the research alone would take a *long* time and I really wasn't looking to do a "list-type" book (that's already been done before). My goal was to dive deep into several cases and give them the perspective and analysis they deserved. I was also curious about the lives of the victims, which are often overshadowed by salacious 24/7 news coverage. Oftentimes, the gruesome details of the murders outweigh the valuable lives of the victims.

As I plugged along on my research, I came across a string of unsolved murders from a few decades ago, also known as the "Madtown Murders." While it continues to grow every year, the Madison area is considered a safe Midwestern hamlet, shielded from some of the more violent crimes of neighboring Milwaukee and Chicago. Madison is a quaint college town known for football on Saturday afternoons in the fall, beautiful recreational lakes, and world-class medical facilities.

It's not known for murders.

What struck me was most of these women were abducted, killed, and in the case of a few of the victims, discarded in remote areas around the city. Six of the seven cases occurred between 1976-1982. Two of them happened on the UW-Madison campus fourteen years apart. It's been forty years since the last murder on the large college campus (as of this writing), which makes one wonder if the two in the late '60s and early '80s were somewhat related.

With more cases—some even older than the ones profiled here—being solved, I couldn't help but think, *Why haven't these seven cases been solved?* While the lost and discarded evidence certainly plays a factor, it goes much deeper beyond that. Each case has its own unique complexities, and it was fascinating to discover the many roadblocks detectives faced while trying to crack these mysteries.

My goal was to interview as many sources as I could, but as I dove into the work, I realized how difficult that would be. Many of the detectives, sheriffs, and police chiefs that worked these cases are long dead and those still alive are well into their eighties. Fortunately, I was able to talk to two detectives that worked on a few of these cases, and they provided what memories they could, digging back into cases from decades ago.

I was also pleased to discuss the cases with current law enforcement officials from the Madison Police Department and retired officers from the Dane County Sheriff's Office.

The UW-Madison Police didn't provide much help, but luckily, I was able to find a bunch of information from old newspaper archives. Since both the Christine Rothschild and Donna Mraz murders happened on campus, they were highly publicized. Suffice it to say, I leaned heavily on secondary sources to find out as much as I could.

While all of these cases are cold, keep in mind they are still open, meaning law enforcement can only share limited information.

I also wanted to reach out to the family members of the victims. I felt, especially early on, it was imperative they got their chance to speak about their loved one's case. I didn't know, however, what would be the best way to get in touch with them. So ... I sat down and wrote them letters. Pen and paper, the old-fashioned way. I tried to explain, as best I could, why I was writing about these cases and that my intention was not to drum up old wounds, but to learn more about the people they tragically lost. Some responded, through email and phone calls, but a few never did. Facebook messages were also sent to a couple of the victims' siblings but were not returned. I decided not to push much beyond the letters. I'm covering a very sensitive subject and if they didn't want to talk, that was totally understandable. At least I gave them the opportunity to do so.

This is my first book. As a journalist and avid writer, I've wanted to write a book for years, but couldn't land on a topic. Nothing seemed the right fit. About five years ago, however, I wrote an in-depth feature story for *Capital Newspapers* in Wisconsin, profiling several cold cases from unsolved murders to disappearances to a strange duffle bag containing the remains of an infant. I really enjoyed working on this piece, and it sparked my interest in writing a book on cold case mysteries. My proximity to Madison, along with the resources I've built up through years of covering the area as a reporter, fired up my passion for this project even more.

While I left a long career in newspapers in 2021, I continued working on the book. The more I poured into the research and the writing, the more these cases enthralled me. Perplexed me. Fascinated me. My interest in unsolved cases actually goes way back to when I was about eight years old. One night, around 1989 or so, I caught an episode of *Unsolved Mysteries* on TV and I was hooked. Spooked for sure. Terrified maybe, but I was fascinated. Between the usual stories of UFOs, Bigfoot sightings, and paranormal activity, the show ran a lot of features on unsolved crimes, especially murders. With help from the show, along with advances in DNA evidence testing, many of those cases have been solved. Unfortunately, many remain cold with few leads three decades or more after the crimes occurred. Where are the people responsible for these vile crimes? How and why haven't they been captured? Questions like these burn inside me to this day whenever I watch classic episodes of *Unsolved Mysteries* or the plethora of true crime documentaries on cable TV.

That's what pushed me to write this book. I needed to learn more about these cases, give them a new perspective, provide new light. While they've been dormant for years, dusting off the case files and bringing them back to public interest could reopen investigations. Maybe one person comes forward with fresh information. Maybe it's the one piece of the puzzle needed to solve some of the most perplexing cases in the history of Madison.

The late, great Robert Stack, host of the original *Unsolved Mysteries*, put it best when he closed out every show with the ominous line, "Maybe you can help solve a mystery."

Chapter 1

Christine Rothschild, 1968

Christine Rothschild awoke at 4 a.m. on the morning of Sunday, May 26, 1968. She was preparing for another normal day.

Rising early wasn't unusual for Chris, a freshman attending the University of Wisconsin. While most college students would rather sleep in, especially on a Sunday, Chris maintained a strict early-morning routine. She would rise early, often before sunrise, to go on a long walk around the large campus in Madison, Wisconsin.

Not only did the walks provide fresh air and exercise, for Rothschild they provided precious time to reflect and collect her thoughts. And she had many thoughts swirling through her mind.

Chris, a bright, studious eighteen-year-old, was nearing the end of her first year of college. She was preparing for finals and working on grueling term papers due in the coming days. Chris was also thinking a lot about her future. That's typical for most college students, but for Chris, something was distinctly different.

She loathed being at the University of Wisconsin.

She had dreams of attending school at a smaller, private campus, perhaps a place like Vassar College in New York. However, her mother Patria had insisted she attend school closer to the Rothschild family's home in Chicago. Chris was furious with her mother and her stubborn stance. In fact, mother and daughter engaged in a fierce argument over leaving Wisconsin the last time Chris visited her family in the middle of spring.

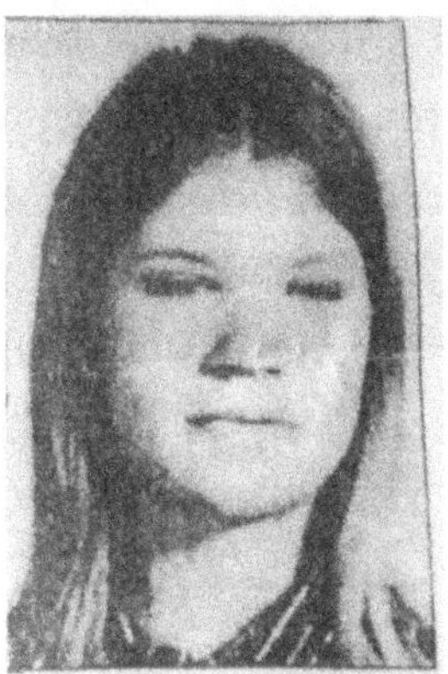

Christine Rothschild

Patria watched her daughter leave home angry and bitter, shouting "I hate you!" before she returned to Madison. Heartbroken, Patria finally relented. Her daughter's happiness was the most important thing. If she wanted to attend Vassar, then so be it.

Chris didn't know of her mother's change of heart as she began her day on May 26.

Her early-morning walks always provided a quiet break from a raucous campus. Yes, Wisconsin is a revered university with high academic standards, but it's also a well-known party school. This tradition was already apparent in the 1960s.

Academically driven and goal-oriented, Chris wanted no part of Wisconsin's party atmosphere. The freshman had big dreams, places to see, people to meet. Chris knew Wisconsin was only a pit stop on her road to bigger life goals.

She was also not into protesting and student unrest.

By the spring of 1968, as the mostly unpopular Vietnam War raged on half a world away, college campuses across the U.S. were a hotbed of protests. As American casualties mounted, students were being called to fight in a war they could care less about. They were tired of seeing friends, family members, and fellow students die in the oppressive jungles of Vietnam.

Wisconsin was no different. In the fall of 1967, a student gathering that began peacefully erupted into violence. Students clashed with police in what became known as the Dow Chemical Protest.

Chris, however, had no interest in marching with students, shouting and waving signs.

While the morning of May 26, 1968 was shaping up to be a tad dreary with cool temperatures, dark clouds, and light rain, it was the perfect opportunity for Chris to get away from all the noise swirling around her.

Anxious to get her day started, Chris stepped out of her room inside Ann Emery residence hall and walked quickly to the bathroom. So quickly, in fact, she almost ran right into Gertrude Armstrong, the hall's night hostess. Upon returning to her room, Chris cracked open a can of spinach and ate a few bites. Pretty, with shoulder-length blonde hair, radiant smile, and petite figure, Rothschild worked part-time as a model for clothing stores in

Chicago. She enjoyed the work and ate healthy to keep her slim physique. The long, solitary walks also helped her burn calories.

Chris dressed for the weather with black boots, black gloves, a mini-dress and a three-quarter-length beige coat. She also made sure to grab an umbrella. A conscientious person, Chris was well-prepared for most situations. But as she walked out of Emery Hall for a normal routine at the beginning of a seemingly normal day, nothing could prepare for the horrible fate that awaited her.

Home Life in Chicago

Christine Rothschild's homelife, growing up at 6338 N. Kenmore Ave. on Chicago's northwest side, wasn't unlike most upper-class students attending UW-Madison.

Most, however, probably didn't grow up in a 15-room house. This was Rothschild's life as a child, one of four daughters raised by parents Emanuel and Patria Rothschild. Roxanne came first, followed by Christine, Arlene, and Suzanne, the youngest.

Financially, Emanuel had done well for himself and his family as a businessman, well-known in the Chicago area. As company president, he led Emro Distributors, a firm that built parking lot gates, and also guided the Factory Trading Post, a business brokerage firm. Both Emanuel and Patria wanted the best for their children and had the means to provide a strong head start.

Emanuel was especially close to Christine, or Chris as most of her friends and family called her. Out of all his daughters, Emanuel felt Chris was going places in life.

Arlene, just hitting her mid-teen years when Chris left home to attend UW, also had a special bond with her older sister. In her book *Murder on the 56th Day*, Linda Schulko describes Chris as a mentor to young Arlene. Chris was energetic, talkative, and approachable and it rubbed off on Arlene, fun-loving and free-spirited.

Arlene also admired her sister's beauty and grace. Chris, five-foot-seven and one-hundred and twenty-five pounds, had a slim figure and combined with a warm, welcoming smile, soft eyes, and pretty face, worked as a fashion model in high school for the Carson, Pirie, Scott and Co. department store. She enjoyed the work, and it allowed her to save money for college. Chris' photo was even featured in a *Chicago Tribune* ad.

With her beauty and personality, Chris could have pursued a career in modeling, but she yearned for something more. She felt a strong pull toward journalism. In high school, she dipped her toes into local reporting, serving as a journalist and salesperson for her school's newspaper. Chris also edited a news sheet for teenage models distributed by Carson, Pirie, Scott and Co.

Besides modeling and her budding journalism career, Chris was a busy high school student. She attended Senn High and, according to the *Chicago Tribune*, achieved straight A's throughout high school. Chris served as a student council president, was a member of the National Honor Society, and, in the spring of 1967, graduated fourth in a class of five hundred.

Despite juggling part-time jobs and the rigors of keeping a 4.0 GPA, Chris found time to assist other students, often helping those behind on their homework. Chris brought that caring nature with her when she came to UW.

While going to college at a large, public university wasn't her first choice, Chris hit the Madison campus with gusto. She enrolled in the Integrated Liberal Studies (ILS) program in September 1967, but after a week of attending classes, something felt off. Chris quickly transferred out of the ILS program and into a general letters and science curriculum. She decided her major would be English. Her freshman classes included anthropology, English, French, and astronomy.

Chris' older sister, Roxanne, was also passionate about fashion. Roxanne, twenty-four years old in the spring of 1968, was a student at the Chicago Art Institute of Design. As a freshman at UW, part of Chris' wardrobe consisted of her sister's designs.

Emily Shannon, a freshman from Wausau who also lived in Emery Hall, told the *Capital Times* newspaper in Madison that Chris "had darling clothes—the cutest I ever saw. I told her so, and she laughed that they were mostly 'rejects' from her sister, who's a designer."

Chris focused on her studies at UW, much like at Senn High. She was admitted to the university's honors program, impressing Dean C.H. Ruedesilli, who told the *Wisconsin State Journal* that Chris was "a very bright student with good ability and determination."

Chris didn't have many close friendships as her first year of college moved along, but she was friendly to almost everyone she met. Not until Linda Tomaszewski came along. Tomaszewski, also a first-year student at UW, met Chris early in the fall of 1967 at South Hall. The two students immediately clicked.

Tomaszewski, currently married, goes by Linda Schulko. She's in her early seventies and lives in Fort Worth, Texas.

"I was drawn to her kindness and caring manner," Linda said in a 2021 interview. "She never hesitated to put another student's needs in front of her own, and always made time to listen to problems in a non-judgmental manner."

Having been raised in the Christian Scientist faith, Chris believed everyone was inherently good in the eyes of God. This led her to help others who were struggling. Similar to tutoring classmates in high school, Chris tried to assist students at UW who had fallen into the grip of drug addiction. She was there to listen, lend support and some guidance to students who often faced their battles alone.

"Few knew that she counselled several heavy drug users on campus in her typical non-judgmental way," Linda said. "Her First Church of Christ Scientist background led her to believe that all people were innately good, promising, and salvageable."

Because Chris carried herself in a confident, non-cocky demeanor, and despite being attractive, bright, and sociable, she did not intimidate fellow students. Friends described her as modest and studious.

"Female students were not jealous of her because Chris never bragged and never flaunted," Linda said. "She was confident in her own skin. Male students quickly saw her as the epitome of high moral standards but were drawn to her goodness."

While Chris tried to keep a laser-focus on academics and helping other students, the atmosphere around her was ripe for distraction. Besides anti-war protests ramping up on campus, UW students loved to party with plenty of beer and, oftentimes, recreational drugs. Wisconsin's drinking culture certainly didn't shun college partying, and for students from other parts of the country, it signaled a welcome reprieve from exams and term papers.

Chris did not share this sentiment, and in Linda, she found a friend who also didn't believe in wasting her time at UW doing keg stands and bong hits.

"She and I were very serious students on a very social campus," Linda said. "We wanted to be scholars and ideally play some positive role in our post-graduation world."

Instead of hitting the nearest house party, Chris and Linda spent free time walking together through the UW Arboretum and Picnic Point, perfect settings for friends who loved nature and animals.

"We would often walk for hours and sometimes seldomly talked," Linda said. "Chris was pensive and quiet and had a calming effect on me. It sounds weird but I think we felt mutual harmony much like yin/yang, although I knew nothing of Asian philosophy in those days. She didn't gossip and needed a release from the campus activity and mayhem. Silence reinvigorated her."

Personality-wise, Chris and Linda were far apart. In college, Linda said she was opinionated, mouthy, and saw everything in black and white elements. She never believed in that gray area of thinking Chris embraced.

"I loved UW, and she hated it," Linda said. "She had deep religious beliefs, and I floundered as a Catholic."

After her shocking murder, Emanuel, Chris' dad, told the media she "apparently loved school at Wisconsin." This could not have been further from the truth. Chris wanted to escape the chaos. She wanted a smaller, private setting where academics were more important than partying, sex, drug use, protests, and riots. She wanted a place far from UW. She wanted Vassar College.

Whether Emanuel truly believed his daughter was happy at UW or was simply trying to put a positive spin on her time there will likely never be known. He died in 2003. Linda contends in her book that her friend wanted to transfer, which led to a heated argument with her mother, Patria. Her outstanding grades, pleasant demeanor, and willingness to help others make it difficult to believe Chris was miserable at UW. She even found a church home, attending services regularly at the First Church of Christ Scientists on Wisconsin Avenue in Madison.

One thing is for certain, she didn't agree with certain attitudes on campus.

During her freshmen year, Chris penned a poem, entitled, "You Are a Sad Campus, Wisconsin," citing her distaste for certain campus activities.

You have to have your beer to promote alumni cheer.
You have to have your sex or else you'll throw a hex.
Stupid, stupid campus, don't you see your loss?

Like almost everyone, Chris had her share of minor vices. She smoked frequently and, according to Linda, loved a strong cup of coffee, hold the cream and sugar. Charged up on caffeine and nicotine, Chris often had trouble sleeping. Her restlessness led to early-morning walks.

During those walks, she often stopped at Rennebohm Drug Store, either on University Avenue or the State Street location. UW students affectionately called the shop, "Rennie's," and besides serving as a pharmacy, the store served coffee, snacks, and fountain soda drinks.

Surprisingly, Chris and Linda never ate a meal together. There were times that she ate in front of Chris, but her friend never took a bite. Linda would often see her purchase laxatives from the drug store, along with packs of cigarettes. Linda said Chris "lived on coffee, spinach, and cigarettes."

This led Linda to believe Chris had an eating disorder.

"I knew something was wrong because she was never hungry, was never tempted to purchase candy bars, chips, soda, and the other junk foods that sustained students between meals," Linda wrote in her book. "She would brush off my concerns with a smile and change the topic."

Linda wrote that Chris had been a "chubby kid" and faced teasing about her weight. Chris also might have felt pressure to maintain her slim figure to secure future modeling gigs. Linda noticed Chris often slept poorly and chose to burn off anxious energy with morning walks around Lake Mendota, which hugs the western edge of campus. Her bouts of insomnia also explain her penchant for coffee and cigarettes, fueling up on stimulants to power through classes and long hours of studying.

Linda was concerned for her friend but didn't want to press the issue until she found out Chris was suffering from a bout of colitis. After weeks or ignoring the pain, she finally went to see a doctor and was prescribed medicine to reduce the discomfort. Linda said Chris' life went "back to normal." However, that would change. On the horizon were more menacing problems to deal with.

Acquaintance Turned Stalker

Sometimes, during her morning walks, Chris would stop to chat with a group of UW Hospital employees enjoying an outdoor smoke break. The group typically met at a side entrance, away from the public entering the hospital.

Chris would puff on a smoke and make small talk. Most of the staff that smoked with Chris were warm and friendly, except one middle-aged surgical resident who seemed somewhat ... odd.

Niels Bjorn Jorgenson, in his early forties in the spring of 1968, had taken an interest in Chris. Tall with wavy blond hair and somewhat charming, he wasn't ugly but Chris showed no mutual interest. She was an eighteen-year-old college freshman. Sure, she had been on a few plutonic dates with college guys during her time in Madison, but they often ended with a peck on the cheek and a hug. Chris wanted her focus to remain on her studies, not men.

Around Chris' smoking pals, Jorgenson was awkward, often bragging about his career in medicine. He apparently didn't smoke but chided those in the group who did. Most of the smokers thought Jorgenson's narcissistic attitude was annoying but mostly ignored the surgical resident. While Chris was cordial toward Jorgenson, Linda said her friend never led him on to think there could be a romantic relationship. She felt Jorgenson was "way too weird."

"I was worried about Niels from the first time Chris mentioned him showing up at her smoke breaks with hospital staff," Linda said. "She was not comfortable around him and strongly disliked how he belittled her smoke break friends and boasted about himself. Being Chris, she was non-confrontational and would not have told him to 'F off,' as would have been my response."

In her book, *Murder on the 56th Day*, Linda wrote that Jorgenson arrived in Madison late on March 31, 1968 and began his residency at University Hospital the following day. He lived with a fellow resident, David Quanbeck and Quanbeck's fiancé, Anita. Linda claims Jorgenson met Chris shortly after he came to Madison. Interest in a much younger woman turned to infatuation, which morphed into stalking.

Jorgenson asked Chris out on a date but was denied. Around this time, Chris started getting prank phone calls to her dorm room. She would pick up, yet no one would answer. Jorgenson would show up at one of Chris' favorite places to study, Memorial Library, following her around when she went on smoke breaks. She also confided in Linda that she believed someone was following her from the library back to her dorm at Ann Emery Hall.

"Shortly after his first appearance at the early morning smoke group, he started appearing in front of classroom buildings when she would enter and leave," Linda said. "He also started sitting in the reading room at Memorial Library a few rows away facing her and following her to the catalogue room and bathroom."

One night, while getting ready for bed, Chris saw a

man standing motionless near a patch of bushes, looking up at her dorm room window. Was it Jorgenson?

While Chris told Linda about the "weird old man" following her, the two friends laughed it off, believing Jorgenson was just love sick. His attention would likely get pulled to another young co-ed before long. Chris' behavior, however, changed in early May. She no longer joked about Jorgenson. She started thinking his infatuation was becoming a serious problem.

"By the time he started standing outside near her window at Ann Emery Hall, I told her to report him to the campus police. We didn't have the word 'stalking' in those days, and harassment just didn't fit since he wasn't actually talking too often to her and never blocked or threatened her," Linda said. "Consequently, Chris didn't feel she had a sound reason to report him. However, once he started phoning her repeatedly, she took action."

In her book, Linda wrote how stalking, especially in the 1960s, was relatively unheard of and not taken seriously by police. That could explain why, when Chris approached two UW police officers about Jorgenson's behavior, she was mostly brushed aside. She told them she wanted to file a report against him. She was allegedly told by one of the cops to "buy a whistle." Linda maintains a report of Chris' stalking complaint was never filed by campus police.

Less than a week later, Christine Rothchild's body, brutally stabbed and beaten, was found outside Sterling Hall.

Violent Attacks Raise Student Concern

About the time Chris was becoming acclimated with student life at UW-Madison, a rash of violent muggings began spreading in and around campus.

The attacks started in September 1967 and intensified as the school year wore on. By late May of the following year, forty cases were reported to UW police. The attacks included street muggings, robberies, and assaults, targeting both male and female students.

UWPD Chief Ralph Hanson told the *Wisconsin State Journal* that, "Fifty percent of the beatings have been resolved, either by closing the cases or by convictions." In some of the street attacks, victims declined to press charges. Campus police, working with Chancellor William H. Sewell, beefed up security and added more police personnel at UW-Madison to protect students, but only after Chris' brutal murder.

Late Saturday night on May 25, just hours before Chris took her last breath, Albert Shade Jr., twenty-three and his wife, Maxine, twenty-two, were attacked as they were walking along the 600 block of University Avenue. Three young men, reportedly in their late teens, approached the couple. One grabbed Maxine Shade and the other two assailants followed suit.

To protect his wife, Shade Jr. tried fighting off the three men, but was outnumbered. His wife broke free, ran into a nearby restaurant, and called the police. As the men continued to beat her husband, Maxine ran out and yelled "the police are on their way!" The three attackers stopped and darted off into the night.

Shade Jr. suffered a mild concussion, several facial bruises, and a chipped tooth in the melee. In the May 27 edition of the *Cap Times*, the same day Chris' murder was reported, the paper stated two of the men in the attack were questioned by Madison police and the Shades intended to press charges.

A day later, a twenty-two-year-old man from Marshall, a small town east of Madison, was dragged on the city's east side, beaten over the head, and had his wallet stolen. David Burks, another Madison man in his early twenties, also reported that "four or five teenage men" jumped from behind a vehicle, assaulting him and his wife for several minutes before fleeing in a car.

A Madison secretary reported about 15 attackers went after her and a group of three friends while walking in the campus area. In another attack, a UW student was slashed above the eye with a razor after being assaulted by six men he said were "older than high school age."

The bizarre rise in attacks, combined with larger, more violent incidents, such as the Dow Chemical Protest in October 1967, the firebombing at South Hall on May 18, 1968, and Chris' shocking murder a week later, forced the university to act. While UW President Fred Harvey Harrington said the freshman's homicide didn't directly affect the university's board of regents to consider increasing the size of UW's police force, Chris' murder was the tipping point. It gave students, along with state lawmakers, ample reason to push the university to get serious about crime on campus.

However, students also cited a communication gap between them and the city police. On Wednesday, May

29, Madison Mayor Otto Festge called the Mayor's Citizen Advisory Committee in for a special session to address the rise in street violence around campus. There was fear a group of rowdy male teens were targeting "hippies," but Madison Police Chief Wilbur Emery said in the meeting students could be overreacting. He said out of forty-five attacks in the city since April 1, only fourteen involved UW students.

"The evidence does not show any organized movement to pick on any particular group, including hippies," Emery told the *State Journal*.

To defend themselves, a group of UW students started a vigilante group to protect a housing area west of the Capitol Square. The mere presence of the group, along with many victims choosing not to cooperate with city police, frustrated Emery, who believed the incidents should be handled by trained officers.

Paul Soglin, a graduate student at the university, was serving on the city council as an eighth-ward alderman. Soglin, who by the spring of 1968, was already known as a student leader during protests on campus, would become a three-time mayor of Madison before leaving politics in 2019, was quite outspoken during the committee meeting.

Soglin claimed students' trust and confidence in city police to protect them had eroded. He called the attacks "hit and run" affairs that happen so quickly, victims don't have time to call for assistance.

The young politician said a group of men, often age seventeen to nineteen, were primarily responsible for the muggings, provoked by community attitudes toward UW students based on their appearance and dress. The suspects attacked students with long hair and beards. Soglin was clearly fed up, opting to work with a group of students to address the rise in violence rather than UW officials.

"We will act as our own spokesman to deal with the Madison community," Soglin said.

While admitting there were some concerns over the attacks, Hanson said it was only a twenty percent increase over numbers from 1967. Hanson said with a campus of nearly 35,000 students, the uptick in incidents wasn't something that was spiraling out of hand. To hopefully stem the tide of violence, UW police added more officers to the lower portion of campus.

Validating Soglin's assertion of a rift between UW students and the city of Madison, Fourth Ward Alderman Gordon Harman suggested students should worry more about cleaning up their dress and attitudes instead of patrolling the streets they called home.

One week later, the Mayor's Advisory Committee passed a resolution calling on Mayor Festge, Emery, Hanson, and the UW administration to "bring all the forces at work in their offices to stop what is becoming a substantial increase in crime on the streets."

Who were these "ad-hoc gangs" of teenage males preying on college students and young professionals? Nonetheless, they needed to stop. Punishment for the crimes needed to increase. Dane County District Attorney James Boll told the committee that in court he would "recommend maximum penalties for offenders and see what we can do to end this."

At the committee hearing, Anotole Beck, a university math professor, believed there was a rise in animosity toward out-of-state students. Beck, finishing his twelfth year teaching at UW, said he had "never seen students so afraid" and had "never seen so many beatings."

Christine Rothschild was from Illinois.

On the heels of a few protests that careened into violence, and the rise in hippy culture with students speaking out against the war in Vietnam, Madison residents outside the campus looked at students with a wary eye. While agreeing with Beck to a point, one committee member said city residents feared students based on recent actions.

Christine Rothschild, despite being an out-of-state UW student, certainly didn't fit the mold of a long-haired, pot-smoking, war-protesting hippy. But, Chris' appearance as a pretty, affluent, intelligent, well-put-together academic might have been enough to stoke the fires of animosity for local teenage boys hell-bent on knocking the "high-brow UW student" down a peg.

Was one of these young men angry enough to kill her?

A Murder Rocks UW Campus

Phillip Van Valkenberg was hoping to spot a friend and fellow co-worker when he approached Sterling Hall on the evening of May 26, 1968.

Van Valkenberg, a twenty-two-year-old UW maintenance worker, found the doors to the physics building's front entrance locked, not unusual for a Sunday night. Not deterred, Van Valkenberg decided to peer through a large window near a clump of bushes to the right of the Sterling Hall entrance. He figured he would see his buddy, tap on the window, and his friend would come around to let him in.

Instead, what he discovered in those bushes was probably the biggest shock of his young life.

Van Valkenberg stumbled upon a grisly scene: The body of a young woman—stabbed 14 times—violently strangled and left for dead. The woman's black gloves were stuffed into her mouth. At about 7:30 p.m., authorities were called to the scene.

For the UW-Madison police force, a department not accustomed to violent crimes, the scene took officers' breath away. Perhaps more shocking was the victim, eighteen-year-old freshman Christine Rothschild. UW Police Chief Ralph Hanson was one of the first officers to arrive on the scene.

"I don't know what kind of person would have done this," Hanson told the *Capital Times*.

Since she was found fully clothed, police didn't believe Chris was sexually assaulted, but part of her clothing was ripped and askew. It was later determined the killer tore out part of the lining of Chris' coat and strangled her with it.

Was Chris killed near the bushes in front of Sterling Hall and dragged to the location where her body was found? Or, was she murdered exactly at or very near the location she was found? Hanson told reporters he wasn't sure but said there was "plenty of blood" where the body was located.

Hanson took command of the investigation, calling in both the Madison Police Department and the Dane County Sheriff's Department to assist. The Wisconsin State Crime Lab was in charge of processing evidence.

Dave Zweifel, a young reporter at the *Cap Times* in

1968, reported the gruesome details for the paper's May 27 edition. Zweifel wrote there was speculation among police that "footprints may have been left at the scene because the ground was soft as a result of the rainy weekend."

Initial investigation determined Chris was likely killed several hours before her body was found. It appeared her attacker struck as she was winding down her morning walk. Sterling Hall was less than six blocks from her Ann Emery dorm.

Marv Balousek, a retired journalist who covered crime for several years for the *Wisconsin State Journal*, has a strong feeling Niels Jorgenson killed Chris. Balousek's book *50 Wisconsin Crimes of the Century*, profiles the Rothschild murder, along with other shocking homicides in the state's more recent history.

"The big thing about the Rothschild case is that it was such a loss of innocence for Madison," Balousek said. "Such a shocking murder and seemingly random murder. Well, maybe not so random if the doctor was involved. It just shocked everybody. UW police kind of reorganized after that; they kind of had been just toggling along and doing little things on campus, then they realized something big like this can happen. They started hiring detectives."

Authorities immediately wondered if there were any eyewitnesses. While it was a rainy Sunday, keeping people inside, if Chris was attacked in broad daylight, as suspected, someone had to have seen something. Regardless, investigators knew they were in for an uphill battle from the start.

"This looks like a tough one," an unnamed UW police

officer told Zweifel. "We've got a lot of people to interview and a lot of places to visit."

As the jolting news of Chris' murder spread, the story made headlines across the Midwest. "CO-ED FROM CHICAGO SLAIN," was the bold, all-caps headline splashed across the front page of the May 27 *Chicago Tribune*, one of Chris' hometown papers.

Linda Schulko found out through a radio report.

Linda went home that weekend to escape campus and write an important term paper. She needed a couple of days away to focus. Linda had actually canceled plans to go to a swim meet with Chris the Saturday night before she was murdered. The last time she saw her was the Wednesday before she returned home to her parents' house in Milwaukee.

Working on her paper in the early-morning hours of Monday, May 27, Linda received a phone call from a UW-Madison police officer. At first, she thought it was a prank, but the officer pressed on, asking her a few questions about the last time she saw Chris and whether she knew of any men who had asked her out and were rebuffed. Linda didn't mention Niels Jorgenson. Tired, bewildered by the call, and a bit stressed, she blurted out another student at UW. She said his name was "Neal" and he lived in Sellery Hall.

He never told her why he was calling.

After hanging up, Linda went back to working on her paper. A few hours later, with her parents up, her father turned to a local Milwaukee radio station to hear the latest news. That's when Linda's world turned upside down.

The station reported Christine Rothschild, UW-Madison freshman, had been murdered.

"The world instantly turned grey," Schulko wrote in her book. "I was devastated and numb."

~

Linda wasn't the only student at UW stunned by Chris' murder.

As the startling news rippled through campus, students expressed shock and dismay. The prevailing thought was *If this could happen to someone as sweet and innocent as Chris, it could happen to anyone.*

The glass bubble of safety many students felt on campus was shattered in a matter of minutes by a crazed, depraved individual.

Whitney Gould, a staff writer for the *Capital Times*, summed it up perfectly in his reaction story following the murder.

> *And if anyone still harbors illusions that the UW campus is a serene little enclave, safe from intrusions of the outside world, the illusions are plainly shattered today.*

Police said it was the first campus homicide in ten years. In 1958, a male student killed another student after a verbal fight turned deadly. The murder occurred at the university's Chemistry Building, near Sterling Hall.

While Chris didn't share a room with another student at Ann Emery Hall, many of the one hundred and eighty-six women who lived in the building knew and liked her. They struggled to grapple with the reality that she was now gone. The victim of a heinous act.

At the tender age of eighteen or nineteen, most young adults have a limited experience with death. They might have dealt with the death of an elderly grandparent, or in some rare cases, a parent, but one of their own? To Chris' friends, it didn't seem real.

"Everyone just keeps saying, 'This can't be. I just saw her—I just talked to her,"' Shannon told the *Cap Times*.

In the same story, Gertrude Armstrong, the Emery Hall night hostess thought to be the last person to speak to Chris before her attack, noted how wonderful a person Chris was.

"The world needs more like her," Armstrong said.

As local media rushed to publish reaction stories from UW students, another prevailing thought was *Why her?* Chris didn't seem to have an enemy in the world. The fact that she was known to reach out and help those struggling with addictions and students needing aid in class, only amplified the question ... why her?

After shock wore off, fear set in. There was a psychotic killer out there, roaming the streets of Madison. Add in reports of recent attacks on students, fear around campus was at an all-time high. Students locked their dorm rooms and kept a low profile.

With fear and anxiety washing over campus like a wave, Chancellor William Sewell warned students to stay around lighted areas of campus and not walk alone. Linda, however, recalled no residence hall meetings, at least not at her Witte Hall dorm. No discussions with students on how to be safe walking on campus. No invitations for grieving students to meet with counselors.

"None of the housefellows, including mine, held a floor meeting after her death and nothing was said in any of my classes about security," Linda said in an email. "No posters from UWPD were on the poles or building entrances encouraging security either. Off campus, friends knew nothing about the murder until hearing city news."

As detectives searched for motives, one prevailing consideration came to the forefront. Could a jilted lover have lashed out and killed Chris? That explains why the detective who called Linda questioned her about any possible male acquaintances in Chris' life.

This theory was quickly put to bed, however, as friends and family told investigators Chris hardly dated. Sure, she would go out with a guy for a formal once in a while, but she kept her relationships platonic. Chris was too focused on her studies to jump into a serious relationship.

Greta Pitkin, a student guidance counselor, told Dane County Sheriff's Office detectives Chris was "very modest, studious, and very attractive."

Chris' parents, Patria and Emanuel, told the *State Journal* their daughter was looking forward to finishing school, returning to Chicago for the summer, and working. The Rothschilds were an affluent family. Chris didn't need to work to save up extra money for school, but insisted. She felt it was time for her to chip in.

"We didn't want her to work, but she was adamant, saying that 'Daddy has paid the bills long enough,'" Patria Rothschild said.

The *Chicago Tribune* printed a lengthier interview

with Patria, noting Chris planned to sell some of her art at fairs and work on writing during the summer. She wanted to keep honing her journalism skills.

"Writing was her field," Patria told the *Tribune*, mentioning a few of Chris' poems had been accepted by a national poetry association.

She was a young woman with bright dreams on the horizon. Chris was determined to succeed.

"Everything she touched was successful," her mother said.

No Suspects, No Motive, No Weapon

With the shock of Chris' murder hanging in the warm spring air of Madison, detectives pushed on, hoping to quickly solve the case and bring the killer to justice.

It would not be easy.

Two days following the attack, police were extremely baffled and frustrated. They lacked a suspect, murder weapon, and a motive. Police did, however, get new information on how Chris died after an autopsy was completed by Dane County Coroner Clyde "Bud" Chamberlain Jr.

The results were ghastly.

Chris had suffered fourteen stab wounds in her chest and neck, was strangled by a piece of cloth ripped from the lining of her coat, had a broken jaw from a direct punch to the chin, and four broken ribs, likely caused from the stabbing. Chamberlain said a puncture wound to the heart, likely from a sharp instrument, was the fatal blow. There was no proof of sexual assault.

If sex wasn't a motive, robbery wasn't either. While

her clothes were askew and jacket ripped, everything Chris was wearing stayed intact. She didn't carry a purse, only a plastic case for cigarettes and her Emery Hall room key. The *State Journal* reported Chris had an "expensive" ring on each hand when she was found. The killer apparently had not taken anything of value.

Hanson, the UW police chief, said the autopsy showed no signs of bruising to her legs, hands, or arms. Hanson said the blow that fractured the student's jaw was likely a "straight-on punch from a fist." It's possible Chris was startled by her assailant, tried running into Sterling Hall for safety, was grabbed, and punched hard in the face, rendering her unconscious.

She barely knew what was coming, which would explain the lack of defensive wounds on her body.

The autopsy couldn't confirm the exact time of death, but Chamberlain thought it occurred before 10:30 a.m. Robert Nolte of the *Chicago Tribune* wrote time of death was around 4:30 a.m. Chamberlain implored that anyone with information should come forward and talk to investigators. Initial clues were vague and didn't provide concrete leads. One female student thought she saw Chris leaving through a side door at Emery Hall at approximately 10:00 a.m. Her body was found less than a mile from her dorm, so it's possible she could have walked to Sterling Hall with her attacker striking around 10:30 a.m.

Another clue came forward days after the murder that Chris was dead by early afternoon. A couple from Waukesha, a Milwaukee suburb about an hour east of Madison, decided to take a stroll through campus on that cloudy, drizzly Sunday. Their small child was being antsy, and they believed a long walk would calm him down and tire him out.

Walking near Sterling Hall, the boy pointed out a "body" near a line of shrubbery outside the building's main entrance. Considering the sophomoric mind of college students, the couple paid little attention to the "body," figuring it was a mannequin, some type of twisted student humor. They didn't report the sighting to the police. That was around 3:00 p.m.

While the crime scene didn't offer a lot of evidence, what was found was shipped to the national FBI Laboratory in Washington, D.C. FBI analysts would test the evidence, cipher what they could from what was available and report back to authorities in Madison. In 1968, DNA evidence testing was not even heard of but forensics analysis was available.

The *Chicago Tribune* reported that "several knives and cutting instruments" were sent to the lab, but Hanson later denied this claim. However, Linda Schulko wrote that only a "rusty lab knife" found in the bushes near the crime scene was sent to Washington. She also claimed Hanson, thinking the knife was too dull and not powerful enough to kill Chris, dismissed it as the murder weapon.

Also sent to the FBI were a blood-soaked men's handkerchief, Chris' clothes, a pair of men's stained pants allegedly found in another location on campus, a black umbrella found stabbed into the ground near Chris' body, and other evidence not made public.

Psychopathic Maniac

What type of deranged human being would violently attack and kill a bright young college student outside on campus during daylight hours?

In an attempt to figure that out, Hanson hired Dr. Seymour Halleck, a UW psychiatry professor, to formulate a profile of the killer. But a blunt, to-the-point assessment of the murderer had already been made by Chamberlain, the coroner who examined Chris' body. The person who committed this awful display of violence had to be a "psychopathic maniac."

While Linda dismissed Halleck's psychological make-up of the killer as "basically meaningless," it was clear Hanson was trying everything he could to crack the case. Along with bringing on Halleck and sending evidence to the FBI for testing, Hanson sent two detectives, Charles Lulling from the Madison Police Department, and Richard Josephson from the Dane County Sheriff's Office, to Roth-schild's Chicago home to talk to family members.

Besides bringing in investigators from Madison and Dane County, Hanson also worked with departments in Illinois and Milwaukee to hunt down possible leads. In 1966, Valerie Percy, daughter of Illinois Sen. Charles Percy, had been attacked and stabbed to death in her bedroom in the family's Kenilworth home.

Closer to Madison, the murders of twenty-year-old Diane Olkwitz from Menomonee Falls in 1966 and sev-enteen-year-old Ellen Kaldenberg from Kenosha in 1967 were still unsolved. The area between Menomonee Falls, Madison, Kenosha, and Kenilworth forms a geographical triangle. Was it possible all the murders were the work of one person, hunting down young women in southern Wisconsin and northern Illinois?

Similar to Emanuel Rothschild, Charles Percy was considered well-off. The Percy family also lived nearby the Rothschilds, on Chicago's affluent northwest side. After his daughter's murder, Percy offered a $50,000 reward (more than $292,000 in 2021 dollars) for information leading to a conviction. As of 2023, the case remains unsolved.

All four victims had not been sexually assaulted and none of their clothes had been removed. While there were distinct similarities in both cases, Hanson hesitated to directly tie Chris' murder to the Percy case or the Olkwitz and Kaldenberg cases. There simply wasn't enough hard evidence to make the connection.

Meanwhile, back at UW-Madison, police were looking for a possible suspect. A white man, around thirty years old with bushy black hair had reportedly been trying to lure young women into his car. It wasn't much, but at least something to pursue.

Hanson and the UWPD kept fielding calls from the public, but no solid evidence or leads came forth.

Were there no eyewitnesses? Did somebody see something? Anything? If Chris was killed in the pre-dawn hours and considering May 26 was mostly an overcast, rainy day, it's possible the murderer struck while it was still dark and most Madisonians were still in bed. But, if she was attacked closer to mid-morning, that opens the door to possible eyewitnesses. While the UW campus is relatively quiet on Sunday mornings, one would think people had to be milling about around 10:00 a.m.

Chris' murder happened directly across from University Hospital, a large medical center. In her book, Linda makes the case that some employees at the hospital must have seen something, but never reported it to the police. A hospital of that size always has nurses, doctors, and other staff members working all hours of the day, even on Sundays. It's odd no one would have seen anything.

Meanwhile, the *State Journal* posed the same question—were there witnesses? In an editorial on May 29, headlined "The Murder at the University," the paper implores anyone with a shred of information, to come forward. The editorial said the shocking murder severely rattled the peace of mind many Madison residents and university students enjoyed in the quaint Midwestern city.

> *But there lingers the possibility that some people may be reluctant to approach the police because they 'don't want to get involved' ... we would remind those persons who 'don't want to get involved' that they already are involved. The entire university community and the entire city are already involved.*

The editorial emphasized that if any persons were around Sterling Hall on the morning of May 26 to "search their minds carefully and try to remember any fact, any bit of information that might be useful to police."

Hanson, in an interview with the *Capital Times*, also said he was disappointed that no one working the 7:00 a.m. shift at University Hospitals had come forward with any possible leads.

On the evening of May 29, at a Christian Science

chapel at 5501 N. Ashland Ave. on Chicago's North Side, a funeral service was held for eighteen-year-old Christine Rothschild. The chapel stood less than two miles from the home Chris grew up in, 6338 N. Kenmore Ave. That address no longer exists as the Rothschild's old neighborhood was purchased by Loyola University and converted into campus infrastructure.

On this night, more than five decades ago, a deep sadness filled the chapel. Many in attendance bowed their heads and wept quietly. Besides the Rothschild family, most of the attendees were high school-aged kids Chris knew from nearby Senn High School or college freshmen. At a young age, many were not accustomed to the pain of sudden death or losing a loved one in such a violent fashion. They would never see Chris' warm, friendly smile again.

A bright young light in this world had been lost forever.

~

As the calendar flipped to June, police continued the exhaustive investigation. Hanson, the campus police chief, was frustrated no new leads or suspects were forthcoming, but detectives were pursuing possible persons of interest.

"We need a break, and we need it bad," Hanson told reporters on May 29.

Police had questioned known drug users Chris had counseled, a psychiatric patient, and two male students who offered rides to female students the night of May 28.

Possible leads that the killer was among those groups had been ruled out. Police, however, were trailing a UW student through surveillance. They approached the student about taking a lie detector test, but he declined, asking to consult an attorney before submitting to the polygraph.

The student in question had talked to Chris less than forty-eight hours before she was found dead, according to media reports. The student's roommate told the press the suspect was "roaming around the room," early on the morning of May 26.

A few days after Chris' murder, Hanson brought in top detectives from both the Madison Police Department and Dane County Sheriff's Office to assist in the investigation. Those included James McFarland, a narcotics investigator, and Detective Charles Lulling, both from Madison, along with Sgt. Richard "Dick" Josephson from the sheriff's office. Josephson worked closely with Lulling on the Rothschild case. The detectives started their investigation by interviewing Chris' family and friends in Chicago in late May.

Lulling died several years ago, but Josephson, well into his eighties, lives in DeForest, Wisconsin, about sixteen miles north of Madison. Josephson has been retired from policing since 1989. While details of the Rothschild case are somewhat fuzzy after more than five decades, Josephson remembers detectives from UW, the city of Madison and Dane County working diligently to solve the young student's murder.

Investigators interviewed thousands of sources as weeks turned into months and eventually years since the homicide occurred.

"We were interested in a lot of people," Josephson said in a 2021 interview. "We just never found a solution."

One suspect, however, was of such high-level interest that Josephson and Lulling, along with Dane County Chief Sheriff's Deputy Reynold Abrahams, travelled to New York City to interview him in mid-September 1968.

Niels Jorgenson reportedly left Madison not long after Chris' murder, although the exact date isn't clear. Schulko wrote in her book that Jorgenson was dismissed from his residency at University Hospitals, across from Sterling Hall where Chris' body was found, the day after the murder. He abruptly packed up his belongings and fled to an uncle's house in Michigan.

However, a *Chicago Tribune* story published September 18, noted Jorgenson was dismissed from the hospital in July. The *State Journal* also reported that Jorgenson's three-month residency probation ended on July 1.

While no direct evidence pointed toward Jorgenson, there was suspicious activity. He was hot-tempered the evening before and the morning of the murder. Co-workers noticed Jorgenson was behaving in an "eccentric manner."

Investigators didn't provide this to the media, but his description, early forties, California native, single, allegedly had served in World War II as a machine gun operator in the European theater, all match Schulko's profile in her book. Jorgenson had also bounced around to do surgical residencies at several hospitals in the U.S. and worked in Africa for a period of time.

Local media reported a man matching his description was around Emery Hall about the time Chris was killed. He had walked another young woman back to her apartment from his in the early morning hours.

After leaving Madison and staying briefly in the Detroit area, Jorgenson continued east where he found work in Brooklyn, New York at a large metro hospital. If he indeed remained in Madison for several weeks after Chris' murder, police had a possible suspect right under their noses but failed to bring him in for questioning.

While Jorgenson stayed one step ahead of the police, detectives from Madison were in hot pursuit. Jorgenson seemed like the best lead authorities had in months. They didn't want to pull back the reigns now.

Dane County Sheriff Franz Haas told the *Chicago Tribune* following Jorgenson was "the hottest thing we've had yet."

"The doctor (Jorgenson) was certainly a prime suspect, whom they interviewed. And the fact it seemed to be a surgical instrument was used to stab her; I think there could be a connection there," Balousek, the veteran journalist, said. "I think they heavily suspected that doctor, but he was in New York City by the time they started investigating him."

Hanson, however, downplayed Jorgenson as a prime suspect, telling local news outlets, "he is not a suspect linked to the crime; he's one of thousands we've questioned to learn where they were and what they were doing May 26." Hanson said speculation of Jorgenson being a lead suspect was simply that ... speculation.

On the morning of September 9, Jorgenson was enjoying breakfast at a friend's house when he was approached by New York City detectives. They had staked out the friend's house for days, hoping to catch a glimpse of Jorgenson. They asked the surgical resident if he wouldn't mind coming down to the Tenth Detective District in Brooklyn's Batch Beach section to answer a few questions related to the murder of Christine Rothschild.

Jorgenson agreed.

He requested an attorney be present for the interview, but the lawyer never made it. He got lost and traveled to the wrong New York City precinct. Surprisingly, though, Jorgenson still consented to the interview. Questioned for four hours by both Madison area and NYPD police, Jorgenson denied any involvement in Chris' murder. Jorgenson explained his whereabouts the day of the Rothschild murder, although it's unclear if he stated a specific alibi. He was released.

Still, Madison area detectives were not giving up. Something about the eccentric aspiring doctor didn't seem quite right.

Lulling, Abrahams, and Josephson wanted another crack at the wannabe surgeon. They tracked him down again in Brooklyn and asked if he would agree to more questioning. Jorgenson agreed. After all, saying no would likely show more suspicion. What did he have to lose? In her book, Schulko describes Jorgenson as a very bright but narcissistic man. He felt he could outsmart the police.

But maybe investigators knew something Jorgenson didn't. More intense grilling could lead to him slipping up. Was this the break investigators had desperately hoped for?

"Sometimes, when you talk to the cops, they'll say, 'Yeah, he did it, we just didn't have the evidence.' I know there was a few murders like that," Balousek said. "There was a priest in Dane County (Rev. Alfred Kunz) killed in the '90s where they knew who did it. They tracked him down in Missouri. But they said he 'lawyered up' and they couldn't get any more out of him."

The air of optimism for Josephson and Lulling, however, quickly turned stale. Schulko claims that once Jorgenson was in the detectives' car, he feigned sickness. He requested the officers to take him back to his apartment. When reached by phone in 2021, however, Josephson couldn't recall why Jorgenson asked to be returned home, only that he remembers leaving the suspect in New York.

On September 21, the three Madison area investigators made the long drive back to Wisconsin. Empty-handed.

"I don't think he said too much to us," Josephson said. "That was the end of our involvement and (the case) was eventually turned over to UWPD."

In early October 1968, Josephson was promoted to acting undersheriff and Lulling was assigned to a large arson investigation. That left UWPD as the sole investigative entity on the Rothschild homicide.

Josephson spent thirty-two years with the Dane County Sheriff's Office, including a period as captain of detectives. Through three decades, Josephson worked a "hell of a lot" of cases, but the Rothschild murder baffled him and many of his peers.

"I've always wished we could have solved it," Josephson said, "but we didn't."

In more recent years, Josephson struck up a friendship with Linda Schulko as she's tried to solve her friend's murder. The retired detective has helped Linda as much as possible, but memories tend to become fuzzy after fifty years and hundreds of high-profile cases. Josephson said it's possible Jorgenson committed Chris' murder, but with no hard evidence pointing toward the former surgical resident, an arrest could not be made.

"I can only go on the facts that I have, what I can prove," Josephson said. "There's no definitive proof he did it."

Josephson dismissed Linda's claim Jorgenson discarded the murder weapon in an enclave at University Hospital. The weapon, believed to be a double-edged surgical knife, was never found.

"She's trying so hard to believe it was him," Josephson said. "Maybe it was, I don't know."

Schulko has referred to Josephson as a "just the facts, ma'am" Joe Fridayesque cop, referring to the popular detective in the *Dragnet* television series. While Josephson was friendly and cordial on the phone, even after three decades away from law enforcement, his strait-laced, follow-the-facts demeanor was still evident. When asked if he has any theories as to who killed Chris, Josephson's response was blunt.

"No."

~

As Lulling and Josephson were preparing to travel to New York to talk to Jorgenson, Hanson was anxiously waiting for evidence test results from FBI headquarters.

"I think it's fair to say we're hoping and praying they'll

come back with something that will help us," Hanson told the *Capital Times* on May 30.

Authorities still believed the murder weapon was hidden somewhere in the vicinity of the crime scene or at least in proximity of the UW campus. Hanson had dismissed a knife found at the scene as being too old and dull to be the weapon, but it was reported the knife was sent to the FBI lab.

In early June, investigators re-interviewed Philip Van Valkenberg, the UW employee who found Chris' body. Police wanted to know if a new round of questions would jog a memory loose inside Van Valkenberg's mind. Maybe there was another clue he spotted at the scene that would help.

By June 2 it was clear a tired group of investigators were running out of options. Hanson told reporters he wouldn't hold another press conference until more substantial information came about. The police chief even apologized for the "skimpy" press briefings.

"We have no new leads, no suspects, no one is under surveillance, no one is held for us for mental examination, and there isn't anybody under arrest," Hanson said.

On June 3, UW put up a $5,000 reward for any vital information in the case. A few weeks later it was raised to $6,000, equivalent to more than $47,000 in 2021.

Dr. Seymour Halleck's psychiatric evaluation was also released at this time. While it didn't offer any earth-shattering revelations, Halleck's report suggested Chris was a "randomly selected victim" and, despite what Coroner "Bud" Chamberlain said, the perpetrator might not have been a "psychopathic maniac."

If Halleck's theory was true, and Chris was targeted at random, the case against Jorgenson runs thin. While he didn't know Chris well, they were acquaintances. Halleck's statement would support the theory that one of the hooligans attacking UW students around campus could have done it.

Could it have been someone else police were overlooking?

In early June, investigators questioned a Madison man with a record of mental health issues. They believed the twenty-nine-year-old was spotted at the Memorial Union on campus the day of the murder. A psychiatric report on the man stated he was "capable of violent acts."

The man told police he "could have committed" the slaying.

The *Capital Times* went so far as to classify the mental health patient as the "prime suspect." However, even as a court order allowed detectives to review the man's mental health history, a legitimate case against him seemed paper thin. Police lacked any hard evidence to further pursue the suspect. While he said he "could have" been responsible for Chris' death, the statement was likely dismissed as nonsense from a person battling mental health issues.

By July 4, as more "confessions" came in, Hanson said investigators were dismissing several claims from "mental patients and cranks."

Meanwhile, the toxicology report from the FBI returned to Madison. It revealed Chris was likely killed within an hour after leaving Emery Hall. She had eaten half a can of diet spinach in her dorm room before going on her customary early-morning walk. Hanson said she was probably killed before 10:00 a.m. since she had not attended services that Sunday morning at the Church of Christ on Wisconsin Avenue, a church she regularly attended.

By late June, detectives still had more than one hundred people to question, but with students gone on summer break, this made questioning more difficult.

Grinning Molester Strikes Campus

As if the campus wasn't already rocked by the Rothschild murder, a killer on the loose, and the uptick in violence against students, a strange "grinning man" began molesting female students.

On June 25, the *State Journal* reported a young man, between the ages of twenty-five to thirty, about five-foot-nine and weighing one hundred and sixty pounds, had grabbed six students and fondled them. While none of the women were injured or robbed, the shock of the attacks was traumatizing. Each molesting lasted less than thirty seconds and after victims screamed and fought back, the grinning fool ran off.

Hanson told the *State Journal*, "He never says anything and there is no evidence that he carries any kind of weapon. He approaches them with a foolish grin, like he enjoys hearing them scream, and grabs them."

Two male students chased the mysterious man after one attack but couldn't catch up to him. He seemed to have a strong knowledge of the layout of campus buildings. The suspect's description matched a man that police were looking for in the sexual assaults of two female students shortly before Chris' murder.

Newspapers ran a sketch of the suspect. There was no question investigators were pinpointing him for questioning in the Rothschild case. Hanson said the rape attacks occurred near Sterling Hall where Chris was killed and both victims were known to walk along fringe areas of campus, similar to Chris. The rape victims had also been threatened with a knife or the perpetrator threatened to use a knife. Both attacks happened on weekends, similar to the homicide.

Hanson believed the Rothschild murder was sexually motivated despite evidence showing she was not molested before the murder. It was believed whoever attacked Chris had a history of violence against women. Hanson said, "I think this is the guy we are looking for in the Christine Rothschild murder case."

By early July, police had quizzed several people through lie detector tests, including a suspect in the Valerie Percy murder. All of them passed and were dismissed.

To put another strange twist into the early investigation, a feud between police forces was revealed at a meeting of the City-University Safety Council, recently formed to combat the rise in local violence. Inspector Herman Thomas, from Madison PD, said city police were upset with UW police for bringing in sheriff's office detectives to help solve the Rothschild murder.

"Thomas told the group it would have been more appropriate to call in city police," the *Capital Times* reported.

The feud came off as petty at a time when local police needed all hands on deck to attack the unsolved homicide. Chris' family and friends needed the tri-county task force to keep working together to try to solve the case and avoid bickering.

And as the days and weeks flew by, new leads continued to dry up.

Could Michigan Murders Be Connected?

As the calendar flipped to April 1969, nearly a year had passed since Chris' murder. No arrests had been made. The case was going cold.

But, could a series of unsolved murders in eastern Michigan be tied to the Rothschild case? Authorities in Michigan were perplexed by five murders, dating back to the fall of 1967, all occurring in a similar fashion, near Eastern Michigan University in Ypsilanti and the University of Michigan in Ann Arbor.

One of the victims, a thirteen-year-old girl in junior high was strangled with a cord and had suffered gashes to the stomach and chest. The killer had stuffed a white cloth down the girl's throat, similar to the gloves shoved down Chris' throat. Two other female victims in Michigan, both college students, were found strangled. Both had clothes wedged down their throats. None were sexually assaulted.

Since the cases followed similar patterns, investigators in Michigan believed the killer was the same person. The two other victims included a twenty-three-year-old law student attending the University of Michigan and a sixteen-year-old girl who had dropped out of high school but hung around college-aged friends in Ann Arbor and Ypsilanti. Those murders, however, were not similar to the strangulation and stabbing deaths of the other victims.

Josephson and Lulling were brought back into the Rothschild case and traveled to Michigan to discuss the cases with local investigators.

"There is enough similarity in the cases to make us believe we may be looking for the same slayer," Hanson told reporters.

Before the Michigan lead, detectives had made trips to question people in Indiana and Pennsylvania. Hanson and Paul Radloff from UWPD had also grilled an alleged female attacker in Janesville. Hanson said, "We're checking every possible lead."

As the one-year anniversary of Chris' death hit, local newspapers wrote about progress in the case. Or lack thereof. Irvin Kreisman, a crime reporter for the *Capital Times*, called the Rothschild case "one of the most celebrated murder cases in the history of the state."

The *Cap Times* also noted that no fingerprints were found on evidence tested at the FBI crime lab in Washington, D.C.

On August 6, 1969, it was reported that John N. Collins was charged with one of the unsolved Michigan murders. Investigators doubted there was a connection to Collins and the Ypsilanti slayings and even more of a remote chance he was linked to the Rothschild case.

By the spring of 1970, more than 1,500 people were questioned in Chris' murder. Police had spent countless hours hunting down tips, pursuing possible suspects, such as Jorgenson, only to come up with ... nothing. Despite the frustrations, Hanson remained hopeful. He told the *State Journal*, "We'll never stop searching. Some day that telephone call will come, with a thread of information, and we'll solve the case."

In 1972, after four years had passed without a break, Hanson refused to close the door on the investigation. Early on, and at least through the first several months of the investigation, police believed Chris was attacked by someone she knew. As the years wore on, though, they speculated she was killed at random.

Could a monster who didn't even know Chris have committed such a heinous act?

Another extremely violent attack in the summer of 1972 threw the Rothschild case back into the spotlight.

Elizabeth Flannery, a seventeen-year-old girl, was stabbed more than thirty times–including five thrusts to the throat–by a crazed madman in Portage, a forty-five-minute drive north of Madison. Flannery was rushed to University Hospitals where, astonishingly, she survived. One of the stab wounds narrowly missed her jugular vein.

On Sunday, August 20, Flannery returned home after hanging out with friends. She left again shortly after 11:00 p.m., telling her parents she was going on a bike ride. Flannery was attacked at some point before 1:25 a.m. That's when Herbert Jones, an operator of the Portage sewage treatment plant, found Flannery. He had been called to repair a lift pump and spotted Flannery by a pedestrian railroad underpass along Highway 51. A kitchen knife and a rubber glove were found near the scene.

Who knows if Flannery would have made it without that broken lift pump and Herbert Jones.

Lulling had talked to Flannery days after the attack

but couldn't gain many clues. He knew a link to Rothschild might have been a long shot, but it was a shot worth trying.

By mid-September, Flannery was able to describe her attacker in more detail. A frightening sketch of a young white man with long, shaggy light-brown hair, mouth agape as if he were shouting or screaming, with an intense glare, was printed in local papers. He was about five-ten, one hundred and sixty-five pounds and was around twenty years old.

Lulling told reporters that detectives were looking into a connection between Flannery's attack and the murder of Sally Kandel, a fourteen-year-old girl in a Chicago suburb, and unsolved murders in the Milwaukee area.

Detectives established many links between the Rothschild and Kandel murders, and the Flannery attack:

- All occurred during rainy days.
- Victims were attacked either at night or early morning.
- The attacks were sexually motivated, although none of the victims were assaulted.
- Victims were dragged or pulled into bushes, cornfields, or overgrown areas near main streets or highways.
- The victims were all around the same age.
- They were stabbed multiple times, suggesting the killer attacked in a vicious rage.

Some of the attacks, minus Rothschild's, were close to train tracks. Lulling theorized the killer was a drifter who hitched rides on trains.

Lulling told the *Capital Times*, "The similarities are strikingly important. We're conducting the investigation as if all these cases were related."

In the case of Flannery, she didn't know her attacker at all. If her case was related to Chris,' this strengthens the theory that the UW freshman was attacked at random.

In the winter of 2018, the Portage *Daily Register* published an update (sort of) on the Flannery cold case. Detectives had explored a few fresh leads and conducted new interviews but, as of 2021, the case remains cold, but active, meaning if a tip comes in, detectives will explore it. Dr. Elizabeth Flannery became a clinical psychologist who treats victims of violent crimes.

In the fall of 1975, the *Capital Times* ran a series of articles spotlighting crime in Madison. A sidebar story flashed with the headline: Rumor Persists, Madison Is 'Easy' for Criminals. William Ferris, Dane County sheriff in 1975, said the rise in crime wasn't so much due to a lack of quality police work—blame it on the city's "liberal" views.

Ferris explained, "The city is a more transient, yet still more tolerant, more open, liberal community than many others of this size in the country. This can lure criminals here."

Perhaps the biggest obstacle in the Rothschild case was that there were no witnesses, or if there were, no one was willing to come forward. "If you got a case and you lack sufficient evidence and you don't have a witness, you can see it's pretty hard to get anywhere with it," John Henry, Madison police detective, told the *Capital Times*.

A few days before Christmas, 1975, another crack of

light broke through in Chris' murder investigation. Richard O. Macek, a twenty-eight-year-old McHenry, Illinois resident, had been charged with killing Paula J. Cupit, twenty-four, who worked as a maid at the Abbey Resort in rural Walworth County in southeastern Wisconsin. Investigators thought Macek was hanging around the UW campus back in 1968.

"If he was on the street, where was he?" questioned Detective Lulling.

Macek had long been fascinated with sexual violence. Nicknamed the "Mad Biter," his record traced back to 1966 and included window spying incidents, stabbing a woman near Chicago, and aggravated battery. In 1974, Macek raped and assaulted a maid at a Holiday Inn in a Milwaukee suburb.

After he was arrested on December 5, 1975, Macek was found to have committed another heinous act. In the fall of '74, Macek, after returning to Illinois, murdered Nancy Lossman and her three-year-old daughter in Crystal Lake. In July of 1975, Macek attacked a twenty-year-old woman in Woodstock, Illinois, nearly leaving her dead.

He eventually fled to San Bernardino, California where his two-year spree of rapes, beatings, and murders finally ended in December 1976. Police arrested Macek and he signed confessions to the Walworth County and Wauwatosa attacks. Deemed a sexual deviant, Macek was committed to the Wisconsin Central State Hospital.

Between his confessions and rape and murder convictions, Macek realized his days as a free man were over. The killer would spend his final years wasting away in prison. Macek eventually decided he couldn't bear another day of confinement. On March 2, 1987, Macek was found dead inside his cell. He hung himself with his own shoestrings.

Macek's involvement in the Rothschild murder could be a far cry, but not out of the realm of possibility. He would have been in his early twenties in 1968 and he was known to travel to Wisconsin. Madison wasn't far from his home base in northern Illinois. Also, Chris' murder does match some of the sadistic ways Macek killed his known victims.

For detectives, Macek was worth looking into but was never a serious suspect.

~

As the years wore on, Chris' unsolved murder grew colder. In 1978, the tenth anniversary approached, bringing renewed media attention to the case, but not much else.

Interviewed for a *Capital Times'* article, Emmanuel Rothschild, sounded like a father losing hope. Rothschild told reporter Warren Gaskill, "I don't know whether they (police investigators) will be able to find the person. We can only leave it up to their good judgement. There isn't much I can do."

While a decade had passed, the Rothschild case still perplexed lead investigators. And for detectives who have died since that dark day more than fifty years ago, Chris' cold case would haunt them to the grave.

"These are cases that we go to bed with," Detective McFarlane told the *Capital Times* in '78. "When you work on these unsolved cases, you don't forget them."

Despite nothing concrete, investigators continued to explore ... anything. In early 1977, the UW police checked into a letter involving the case and, later in the year, the Madison police interviewed a man charged with a stabbing homicide, but he was not in Madison at the time of Chris' murder.

In April of '78, Charles Lulling, who worked alongside Dick Josephson in the early weeks of the Rothschild investigation, announced his retirement. Since 1960, as a prime investigator, Lulling had solved around twenty homicides. However, the Rothschild murder was one he simply couldn't resolve.

"We interviewed a lot of people in that case but we never found a solution," Josephson said in a 2021 interview.

Another Viable Suspect?

When it was comes to depraved, few men could be considered more depraved than William Floyd Zamastil.

On June 1, 2004, Zamastil was convicted of killing Jacqueline Bradshaw, an eighteen-year-old, and her seventeen-year-old brother, Malcolm, in a case finally resolved after twenty-six years. He was sentenced to two terms of twenty-five years to life in a San Bernadino, California courtroom.

The *Los Angeles Daily News* reported that on February 27, 1978, Zamastil picked up the siblings who were hitchhiking from Las Vegas back home to Los Angeles after helping a friend move. Along the route, near Barstow, California, Zamastil bludgeoned the two teenagers to death.

Zamastil, who was fifty-two years old in 2004, pleaded guilty to the slayings to avoid the death penalty. In Wisconsin, Zamastil was already serving time for the

August 1, 1978 abduction and murder of a twenty-four-year-old woman in Madison. Zamastil allegedly kidnapped the woman from a department store parking lot, drove about fifteen miles out of the city, raped, and killed her.

In the months prior to Zamastil's conviction for the Bradshaw murders, investigators were working diligently to connect Zamastil to another killing. Zamastil reportedly abducted Leesa Jo Shaner from a Tucson, Arizona airport parking lot and murdered the young woman, daughter of FBI agent James Miller. Zamastil was found guilty by a federal grand jury on July 28, 2011.

Miller worked for decades to bring justice to his daughter's killer. Unfortunately, Miller died in 2007, unable to see Zamastil convicted, but her family could finally enjoy some semblance of closure. They can thank seasoned detective Rick Luell for helping find the killer.

Before being convicted in Shaner's murder, Zamastil was nearing possible mandatory release for the Wisconsin murder. Psychologically disturbed with a thirst for rape and violence, detectives didn't believe years in prison had transformed the troubled Zamastil into a good-natured soul.

"Zamastil was telling other inmates that he couldn't wait to get out so he could rape and kill again," Luell said in an email interview.

Luell, working for the Wisconsin Department of Justice, Division of Criminal Investigation, Cold Case Unit, wanted to make sure Zamastil would remain behind bars for life. Working with a jailhouse informant close to Zamastil, Luell pieced together admissions from the killer. Through letters sent from the informant to the detective,

Zamastil admitted to killing Shaner. There was also a college girl from many years back.

A college girl in Madison, Wisconsin.

Luell began working with the informant at the Waupun Correctional Institution in the 1990s. With every letter received, fascinating bits and pieces of Zamastil's life as a rapist and murderer started coming together. In numerous letters, the informant wrote about Zamastil bragging about killing a young college co-ed.

"In doing my homework, I learned that Zamastil was receiving in-house psychiatric care on the Madison campus and was staying in a residence across the street from where Rothschild was killed," Luell said.

Armed with a major new lead, Christine Rothschild's case file was suddenly cracked open again.

Luell believed Zamastil killed Chris because, through speaking with the informant, he described the case with vivid details. Vital information only the killer would know. He said he jammed his glove down Chris' throat to prevent her from screaming. Indeed, gloves were found stuffed down her throat.

"You would have to have a photographic memory to provide the information Zamastil provided to law enforcement years later," Luell said.

There was one major problem, however, with this credible new lead. Actually, two. Both stem from huge missteps by the UW-Madison Police Department. First, according to Luell, was the mistake of leaking too much information on the investigation to the media.

"There was a problem with all of the detailed information he was providing. It could not be used to convict him. The problem was the UW police chief gave his entire report to the chancellor, who gave it to the press and it was printed. Therefore, Zamastil could always claim he had read the detailed information in the press," Luell said. "This is why the police do not give a lot of information to the press."

It would make a strong defense issue for Zamastil, Luell said. With a mind as warped as his, the argument could be made that he read the details of the Rothschild murder in the paper and either convinced himself he did it or figured it would make a good story for the prison informant.

Despite questioning him on numerous occasions, Luell could never get Zamastil to flat-out confess to Chris' murder.

"Remember, he has psychological issues," Luell said. "Zamastil liked playing with the police. He made many 'admissions' but admissions are not confessions."

The second huge mistake UWPD made in handling the Rothschild case was discarding information. Literally, throwing it out. In an open case.

Surprisingly, discarding old evidence happens more often than one would suspect. Police officers move to other departments, retire, get transferred and, after a few decades there's plenty of staff turnover. A new officer comes in, has no recollection or knowledge of a dated—yet still open case—and tosses evidence they believe could be from a solved case. Evidence rooms, especially before the digital revolution in the 1990s, were stocked, cramped quarters with boxes stacked to the ceiling. Material from old cases were likely pushed to the side and forgotten about for years.

From the time between Chris' murder in the late '60s to technology and scientific breakthroughs in the '90s, DNA testing came a long way. Labs could take a drop of blood, for instance, and trace it back to potential suspects. In the last twenty years, many cases—considered cold and lost to history—have been solved using DNA testing.

"I went to look for the evidence collected at the crime scene and autopsy to see if we could get his DNA from any of the items of evidence," Luell said. "The problem was that the UW police had discarded all of the evidence over time. Therefore, we did not have any evidence to physically link him to the homicide."

There was no way, without a true confession, he could match Zamastil to Chris' murder. And, considering the convicted murderer had severe mental issues, even a confession would be considered suspect. It could be deemed as another bizarre way for Zamastil to brag about committing a horrific tragedy.

"A case is never closed until someone has been convicted," Luell said. "And in this case, it would be a good defense for Zamastil to say he got all of his information from newspapers. I personally don't believe Zamastil got all of his information from the newspapers because he provided too much detail on the homicide."

While Zamastil was receiving psychiatric care in a facility near the crime scene, he would have been sixteen years old in the spring of 1968. Could a sixteen-year-old boy be sophisticated enough to pull off a brazen attack and murder and get away with it? While it seems like a stretch, it's certainly possible. It's likely Zamastil was already having deranged thoughts at a young age, especially if he was getting treatment.

In 2006, UW-Madison Detective Bruce Carroll was assigned to the Rothschild cold case. Talking to the *State Journal* in '06, Carroll believed the murder was a "hurried sort of event."

"I don't think it was well thought out," he said.

That could describe a deranged teenager, panicked and desperate to end Chris' life before screams could be heard. However, that doesn't necessarily rule out Jorgenson, the aspiring doctor and alleged Rothschild stalker, either.

The name Niels Jorgenson does not ring a bell for Luell. The retired detective said Jorgenson's name did not come up when he worked with the UWPD on the Rothschild case as a special investigator.

"I never heard of Niels Jorgenson, so I never investigated him," Luell said. "Remember, I was investigating the many homicides Zamastil was bragging he committed. The UW police must have kept the Jorgensen information to themselves."

The bottom line is, the two most credible suspects in the Rothschild case remain a surgical resident in his early forties and a mentally unstable teenager. Jorgenson, according to Linda Schulko, died on February 16, 2013. He was eighty-seven years old. Schulko corresponded with Jorgenson up until his death, documenting several bizarre letters and phone conversations she had with him in her book. While he never admitted to killing the young college student, his bravado attitude and contempt for the police investigation leads one to think Jorgenson knew too much for an innocent man.

Zamastil, meanwhile, is serving his time at the Waupun Correctional Institution in Wisconsin. With the Shaner conviction, Zamastil will never see the light of day.

No matter who killed Chris, her shocking murder affected many lives on the UW campus, Madison and Chicago, her hometown. In the Rothschild home, family members suffered in silence. Chris' younger sister, Arlene, said the murder–and Chris herself–was rarely discussed.

In a 2006 interview with *Cap Times* columnist Doug Moe, Arlene said her father, Emmanuel, hired a private investigator to hunt down leads in the case. But that only caused more grief for Patria, Chris' mom. Every time the phone rang at the Rothschild home, Patria would jump. The family stopped working with the private investigator.

Arlene told Moe that after her parents died in the early 2000s, she could finally grieve her sister's death. Only a couple of years apart in age, Arlene said Chris and her "were like twins."

As the 40th anniversary of Chris' murder approached, Schulko and Arlene began planning a memorial event at UW-Madison. Hoping to attract new interest in the case, Schulko began corresponding with UW police. She was also hoping the man she suspects killed her best friend–Niels Jorgenson–would show up at the memorial.

Through a series of emails in 2021, Linda said her relationship with campus police started off well enough, but eventually turned sour.

Perhaps she was being too pushy for the department's

liking, or detectives felt they didn't have the energy or manpower to devote time to a forty-year-old cold case. Whatever the reason, the UW police remain mum on anything related to the Rothschild case. Contacted in 2021 for comment on both the Rothschild and Mraz cases, UW Police spokesperson Marc Lovicott, after checking in with detectives, responded with the following:

> *I had a chance to share your email with a few folks at our department. While the cases remain open, they are indeed cold cases and we don't have a cold case unit. We've also had some retirements over the last few years in our detective bureau and we've lost some institutional knowledge about the cases. Simply put, we don't have any staff available who feel comfortable speaking publicly about the cases.*

Around the time Linda was planning the anniversary memorial, she received a startling letter from Reverend Kay Krebs, a pastor in Colorado. Back in 1968, Krebs was working as a student at UW Hospital. She knew Jorgenson and described him as strange and narcissistic. He had only been a surgical resident at the hospital for several weeks but had already earned a reputation for being rough with female patients.

Jorgenson was skating on thin ice at the UW Hospital.

Krebs had read an article Linda had written for a UW alumni magazine about her friend's unsolved murder. Thinking she could help her in some way, Krebs penned a letter that stopped Linda in her tracks.

On the afternoon of Sunday, May 26, 1968, while

working her shift at the hospital, Krebs recalled a very odd conversation she had with Jorgenson. Maybe not a conversation per se, since most staff members who knew the braggadocious resident tended to avoid talking to him. However, it was a comment that remained burned into Krebs' memory for forty years. Noticing the rainy dreariness outside, Jorgenson glanced out a window.

"Nice day for a murder," he said.

Chris had already been dead for several hours. Despite the bizarre comment and Jorgenson's puzzling behavior (he allegedly showed staff members photos of mutilated bodies from a previous residency in Africa), Krebs didn't inform police back in '68.

After she received the letter from Krebs in 2006, Linda handed it to the UW police. Krebs, however, told the *Isthmus* newspaper in Madison that detectives never called her. By 2008, Lt. Peter Ystenes was head of the campus police department's detective bureau. Ystenes told the *Isthmus* that while he wasn't aware of the information from Krebs, the detective assigned to the Rothschild case likely knows about the letter and that the department has "followed up on hundreds of leads, and I'm sure that one was followed up on."

It wasn't.

When an *Isthmus* reporter asked why Krebs wasn't contacted, Ystenes said he "wasn't sure."

Linda also pushed the department to submit evidence to the Vidocq Society. Based out of Philadelphia and formed in 1990, the society is comprised of "seasoned professionals" with backgrounds in law enforcement. The group gets together to discuss cold cases in a social setting.

While they've had success through the past thirty years in solving perplexing cases, they only work cases upon request from law enforcement.

But with evidence from Chris' case spread out among three departments, the UW police, Dane County Sheriff's Office, and the FBI—and with items presumably lost—trying to take on the case would be difficult, even for the Vidocq Society.

Still, Linda never lost hope that her dear friend's case would be solved. Rothschild's immediate family appear to have moved on from any hope that their sister's murderer will be brought to justice. Linda was talking to Arlene, Chris' younger sister, for years and while she was involved in planning the 2008 memorial. In recent years, though, Linda said Arlene has stopped corresponding with her.

Arlene did not respond to a request for an interview for this book. Regardless of Arlene's thoughts about her sister's murder, it's clear from social media posts that Chris is always on her mind, especially when May 26 rolls around every year. In 2021, on the 53rd anniversary of her sister's death, Arlene wrote on her Facebook wall:

> *53 years ago has terrible memories for all of us who knew Christine Rothschild. Today is the day you were murdered and we never forget the love and great memories you shared with us.*
>
> *Thinking of you more than usual today my dearest Christine. I deeply appreciate the 16 years I was blessed to have had you in my life. You left me way too soon. I hold onto your memories fondly and will love you forever and ever...*

~

For some seasoned investigators, like Dick Josephson, it was easier to move on from the Rothschild case. After all, there would be plenty of other cases to dive into. But for others, such as UW police Chief Ralph Hanson, the frustration of not bringing Chris' killer to justice became a nagging feeling that would never go away.

Hanson Deeply Affected by the Murder

Mike Hanson said goodbye to his father more than twenty-five years ago when he died in 1996. Mike was only in his mid-twenties. Take a glance around his office at the Madison Police Department's South District, however, and signs of the late Ralph Hanson are all around.

Bright, vivid oil and watercolor paintings depicting breathtaking scenes from the great outdoors are hung with care. Ralph spent his free time painting. His artistic expression was a relaxing way for him to de-stress from the high-level job of running the UW police department.

"His hobby was oil and watercolors, and I couldn't draw a straight line with a ruler," Mike said.

While Mike may not have his father's artistic aptitude, he did inherit Ralph's passion for community service and helping others. So, at the age of twenty-nine, when most people are settling into their careers, Mike shifted into an entirely new one. He left the private sector and became a police officer.

"He never pushed me to get into law enforcement," Mike said, referring to his dad in 2021. "He said it was a thankless job and that we (his children) could do better. What he did instill is a sense of service. When I was in the private sector, I had this burning itch to have a job with meaning. That's what he instilled in (his kids) was having a job with some meaning in society."

In more than two decades with the Madison Police Department, Mike has served several roles, including as public information officer. He was promoted to captain in 2019.

"He never saw me become a police officer, which is fine," Mike said. "I know he knows now."

From the Dow Chemical Protest in 1967 to the Sterling Hall bombing in 1970, the Vietnam era on the UW campus was especially difficult for Hanson and his officers. The Rothschild murder, however, cut deep to Chief Hanson's core and, as a father, affected him personally. Mike was born after the 1968 homicide, but as a child years later, recalls discussing the case with his father.

After Rothschild's murder was reported to the police, Hanson was one of the first on the scene. The startling images he witnessed that day stayed with him to his grave. Being an experienced cop with a rugged persona, Hanson rarely cried. Tears were shed though when he realized the shock of what happened to Rothschild, a bright, beautiful young student slain in cold blood.

"This case haunted my dad," Mike said. "At the time, he had two of us four kids and he thought 'This beautiful eighteen-year-old daughter is dead and she's somebody's daughter and sister and now she's dead. And she died violently; it wasn't an accident.' I know he did everything he could, at the time, and in the future with whatever new technology became available to solve this and it just hasn't been solved."

From the moment Chris' body was discovered, Hanson, who started his tenure as chief in 1965, was front and center on the case. He told his staff to push off vacations and pool all its energy into solving the homicide.

"Every morning the detectives had to come in, do a briefing on anything new that was learned and then they would dish out assignments as to what they were going to go and tackle for the day as far as follow-up leads, collecting evidence and interviews," Mike said. "It was intense for months and then the case went cold because they didn't have enough to make an arrest."

Balousek said the brutal murder prompted Hanson to reorganize the entire police department because "in Madison, nothing like that had happened before or in a long time anyway."

Upon his retirement in 1990, Hanson told the *State Journal's* Bruce Kaufman that when he came to UW-Madison twenty-five years earlier, the sprawling Midwest campus was "a pretty quiet place."

"It was the last place in the world someone would suspect violence," Hanson said. "Violence on a campus contradicts the very purpose of a university."

Assuming Chris was attacked around sunrise, Mike is perplexed that not a soul heard Chris screaming. Or, if they did, it was quickly ignored. Someone may have decided to not get involved in a potentially violent situation. They could have brushed it off as "not my problem."

"You have to remember, downtown Madison at 1:00, 2:00 in the morning, if you scream, it's falling on deaf, drunken college kids' ears who hear screams all the time, so unless you're absolutely screaming 'I'm being raped! I'm being stabbed!' most people are just going to ignore a scream back then and the same is (true for) the case now," Mike said. "As an aside, a couple of years ago, there was a woman being sexually assaulted right on University Avenue at 7:00 in the morning. This guy followed her, tackled her on the ground, and sexually assaulted her. Car, after car, after car drives by her and finally someone calls 911. We had a cop get into a foot chase with him for blocks and they end up catching him.

"People either don't want to get involved, they turn a blind eye, or they're scared to call police for some reason."

There's also the theory Chris knew her attacker and let him quietly approach. This would support the case against Jorgenson. The young student certainly wasn't friends with the middle-aged aspiring surgeon, but they were acquaintances. And, according to Schulko's memories, he harbored an unhealthy obsession with the pretty blonde freshman.

Reflecting on one of his father's most high-profile cases, Mike Hanson ponders several intriguing questions.

"I wonder if she had a chance, or did he come up behind her and immediately muffle her? Also, where were police? Night watchmen? Where were they at the time? Did they hear anything?"

In the months and years following the Rothschild murder, Chief Hanson made a point of reaching out to Chris' family with updates. While it was reassuring for the family to know the UW police were still actively pursuing leads, it was likely gut-wrenching to the Rothschilds that her killer was still at large. However, the family rarely talked about the case amongst themselves and—somewhat more bizarre—hardly spoke about Chris.

"I was told this by Linda; never were they allowed to talk about Christine after her death, never did they celebrate Christmas again," Mike said. "That's the wrong thing to do, but they didn't know about trauma care back then. Now, we talk about trauma care as you need to talk about it with someone. We need to ask questions and celebrate lives, like Christine's, as heroes and how great people they were. Back then it wasn't like that. It makes me sad."

Ultimately, while his department doggedly pursued thousands of leads, conducted countless hours of interviews, and searched in vain for the murder weapon, Chief Hanson kept coming back to one man: Niels Jorgenson.

"I think he was pretty focused on one suspect based on information that came in," Mike said, referring to Jorgenson. "From what I understand, from talking to his former employees, my mom and others, he was zeroed in on that individual."

This is why Hanson and the Intra-County Task Force sent detectives Josephson and Lulling to New York to question the wannabe doctor. But the lack of a slam dunk piece of evidence tying him to the case—along with Jorgenson's apparent "illness" on the way to the Brooklyn precinct—were roadblocks investigators couldn't overcome.

Nonetheless, Hanson never stopped thinking about the case. In his retirement interview with the *State Journal*, Hanson said the public probably couldn't even grasp how much time his staff put into trying to catch Chris' killer.

"If there's ever information, you'd bet I'll try to develop it," Hanson said. "I'll never give up."

For Hanson, the Rothschild murder wouldn't be the only unsolved mystery involving a female student at UW. Fourteen years later, another violent attack would leave another beautiful, bright young woman dead and shake the campus community to its core once again.

Before that, however, five other Madison-area women would go missing and have their young lives brutally cut short by an unknown assailant. Between 1976 and 1982, fear gripped the capital city.

Chapter 2

Debra Bennett, 1976

Debra Bennett was afraid of dying.

Most people harbor some fear of death and the thought of physically leaving this Earth, but Debbie was petrified of it. She was so afraid of death, in fact, that at nearly twenty-one, she still hadn't obtained a driver's license. She was scared she would kill someone or be killed in a crash.

The thought of her father, only fifty-eight years old, battling terminal cancer also contributed to Debbie's anxiety over death. She knew he didn't have much time left. Knowing he was wasting away and there wasn't much she could do to help weighed on her.

But the young woman was excited to be in a new city. A big city. While Madison, surrounded by small suburbs, cornfields, and cows just outside its city limits, could be considered small potatoes for someone from a major Midwestern hub such as Chicago, "Mad Town" was huge to Debbie.

She grew up in tiny Ridgeway, Wisconsin in rural Iowa

County. After graduating from Dodgeville High School in 1973, Debbie stuck around her hometown for a couple of years. But life in a small town was too serene. Free-spirited and easy-going, Debbie yearned for more. The city brought excitement, new friends, parties, and possibilities. Those are aspects many twenty-year-old women yearn for when they move to a new city, hoping to get their life started.

Debra J. Bennett

However, for Debbie, it would be the beginning of the end.

Her body was found—badly burned and discarded—in a rural ditch near Cross Plains, about twelve miles west of Madison, on July 21, 1976. One day before Debbie's twenty-first birthday. Two farm surveyors, Ronald Williamson, twenty-nine, from Waunakee and Daniel Birrenkott, twenty, from Sun Prairie, had been walking through the area, surveying land when they stumbled upon Debbie's body. The area around her was also severely burned.

The only way detectives could identify Debbie was through dental records, obtained from her childhood dentist, Dr. F.J. Fenske, and a broken collarbone suffered from an injury when she was eight years old by Dr. Billy Bauman, a pathologist from St. Mary's Hospital in Madison.

The fire only made determining the cause of death harder for investigators. While Dane County Coroner Clyde "Bud" Chamberlain Jr. told the press on July 23 that exactly how Debbie died couldn't be established, lead detective Lt. James McFarlane from the Madison Police Department said authorities were "treating it as a homicide until ruled otherwise."

Originally, detectives said Debbie had been missing since July 8, when she was last seen leaving the Cardinal Hotel in downtown Madison. She had been staying there since around July 1. But she abruptly left eight days later without checking out. Luther Getty, the hotel's manager, told the *Capital Times* that he didn't think Debbie stayed in her room at all.

"The day after she checked in, nobody saw her," Getty said. "She apparently died after she checked in. Nobody saw her and nobody really knew her."

Friends described Debbie as quiet, but very nice and sociable. It's possible the young woman, after checking into her room at the Cardinal, was out and about, spending little time in her room. Prior to July 1, she had lived at a residence along Loftsgordon Avenue.

Getty also said social workers had stopped by the hotel to track down Debbie. They wanted to locate her before her father took his last breath.

On July 27, however, it was determined Debbie was last seen July 10, walking barefoot along the west side of the 1400 block of Loftsgordon Avenue on the city's northeast side. The Dane County Sheriff's Office said Debbie was spotted at 7:15 p.m. walking away from the apartment building she had previously lived in. Witnesses told the department Debbie was wearing blue jeans, carrying a denim jacket, and a brown shoulder-strap purse. She was walking barefoot in the direction of Aberg Avenue.

It was a bit odd that Debbie was walking the streets barefoot in the middle of summer. The temperature in Madison soared to 101 degrees that day, three notches off the all-time record. Similar to most Madison residents, Debbie probably needed to get out of her shoes on a blistering hot day.

Debbie had been evicted from her place on Loftsgordon Avenue. She formerly worked at a inn in Madison, but was unemployed at the time of her disappearance. A friend believes she was living off welfare assistance. In June, Debbie had been arrested and charged as a suspect in an apartment burglary on Williamson Street on Madison's near east side. She wasn't convicted of the crime at the time she went missing.

It's clear by the second week of July, Debbie was somewhat down on her luck. She had moved to the big city only half a year earlier but was already struggling. The high hopes and optimism she felt months earlier were diminishing.

And her dad was dying.

For a twenty-year-old trying to make it on her own, it was all a lot to handle. Despite it all, Debbie remained fairly upbeat. She was still going out, having fun, and living life as most young women do. About a week before she was last seen, Debbie attended a concert in Madison.

She spotted a friend and politely chatted; despite being worried about her dad.

The friend, only identifying herself as "Karen," told the *Capital Times'* Floyd Nelson Jr. that Debbie was "really quiet, small built, and very pretty the last time I saw her.

"She didn't deserve to die like this," Karen said. "She was really a good person."

In a story headlined: "'Big City' Wasn't Answer for Small Town Girl," Karen said Debbie was hoping to find excitement and a fresh start when she moved to Madison in early 1976. She wanted something more than what little Ridgeway had to offer. Something bigger, brighter, but not too large like Milwaukee or Chicago, places that could swallow up a small-town country girl.

Madison *seemed* safe.

Still, it was a large enough place where temptation lurked on most street corners. The drug culture was alive and well in the '70s, and Madison wasn't immune. In her effort to meet people and develop friendships, Debbie likely befriended people who didn't have her best interests in mind.

Karen told the *Cap Times,* Debbie enjoyed going out and partying. "She was involved in drugs and a few other things."

Debbie was a sincere, trusting person, though a bit naïve. She was attractive and friendly but didn't appear to have a boyfriend at the time she was killed. Speculations can lead one down a rabbit hole of theories, especially in decades-old unsolved murders. But perhaps Debbie, warm and inviting, had invited the wrong person in. Perhaps she made the fatal mistake of trusting someone she thought she knew. Someone who betrayed her trust and innocence and took her life.

"Debra went straight up and straight down ... now she's dead," Karen said. "She went straight to her peak; whoever killed her was trying to cover-up."

Not much is known about Debbie's hobbies or interests, but she did enjoy poetry. She would often call Karen early in the morning and read her poems. The friends would catch up, laugh, and talk about life. Karen remembers one May morning, just a couple of months before Debbie went missing, when she received a call at 3:20 a.m. *Who would be calling at this time of day?* It was Debbie.

To her friend, she read the following poem:

> *If you must hate me, hate me always and not when you are just upset with life or confused and angry. If you must hurt me leave me, for then I will be hurt only once. Don't lead me on and then drop me. If they love me, let them tell me and not someone else because I need to know. If you don't understand, don't tell me because it's me that doesn't understand. If you would think, you would know that I do love them.*

"Maybe this poem sums it up," Karen said in 1976.

Her friend was a young woman searching for love and acceptance. She yearned to find it in the big city of Madison. It never came.

At first, authorities weren't sure if Debbie's death was a homicide or suicide. Karen said while suicide could be possible in a case of this nature, the theory didn't fit with Debbie. She feared death and had a zest for life.

As detectives continued to put the pieces together, however, it was clear she was murdered. The most baffling thought was whether Debbie was killed somewhere else, dumped off in that ditch along Old Sauk Pass Road, burned, and left there. Whoever did this was extremely cold and callous. They were smart too, knowing that by discarding her body in a very rural area, miles outside the nearest town, it would likely take weeks for someone to discover her remains. Burning the body would also destroy valuable evidence.

Investigation into Debbie's murder was led by a thirty-member group of detectives—the same group that investigated the Rothschild homicide—from the Madison Police Department and Dane County. Due to lack of evidence and no eyewitnesses coming forward, the intra-county unit didn't have much to work with. While frustrating, investigators continued to push forward with any new lead they could find.

Meanwhile, the Bennett family was dealing with another tragedy. William Bennett, Debbie's fifty-eight-year-old father, lost his battle with cancer. He died on July 26, just days after his daughter's body had been found.

After years of struggling, fighting through a horrible disease, Bennett decided to let go. Perhaps he was hoping to be reunited with his daughter.

On the afternoon of July 29, 1976, mourners filed into the Lulloff-Peterson Funeral Home in Dodgeville, Wisconsin. Unlike most funerals, on this day family and friends grieved for *two* beloved souls. Debbie's mother, Marie, along with sisters Connie, Sharon, and Cindie, and

William, a brother, were burying both Debbie and their father on the same day.

~

On Thursday, August 12, more than a month after Debbie had been murdered, a mysterious key was sent to the Cardinal Hotel in Madison.

The key, belonging to the hotel at 418 E. Wilson St., was a room key returned to the Cardinal through the mail. It was Debra Bennett's room key.

A day later, the *State Journal* reported the key "carried the customary hotel key tag asking finders to drop it in a mailbox with return postage guaranteed by the hotel."

The key immediately sparked questions. Who found it? Who dropped it in a mailbox? Was it the person who killed Debbie? Was it a random person who simply found the key and was performing a good deed by returning it? Was it a message from the killer? Was this a sick joke meant to taunt the police?

Almost four weeks had passed since Debbie's body was discovered yet detectives had few leads, zero suspects (at least none made public), or a clear motive. The returned key did open a door, albeit just a crack, into a credible lead.

Investigators wanted whoever found the key to call local police. They wanted to know where it was found and who found it.

Detective Theodore Mell told the *State Journal* that the location of where the key was found could assist the intra-county squad in finding clues to the person responsible for Debbie's death. By mid-August, they had reached dead ends. The key was a sliver of hope.

Debbie checked into the Cardinal on July 1 but didn't hang around the hotel much. Despite being evicted from her apartment on Loftsgordon Avenue, all of her clothes were still there, and she was last seen walking from the complex on the evening of July 10.

Since she hardly stayed in her room at the Cardinal, it's possible the key may have dropped from Debbie's pocket or a purse. Someone could have found it on a Madison sidewalk and shipped it back to the hotel. Then again, it seems odd and somewhat random that the key was returned a month after her murder. Was the killer playing mind games with investigators?

Whoever sent the key never came forward. The mysterious room key remains a puzzling clue decades later.

Drifters Go on Killing Spree

Hitchhiking was prevalent in the 1970s.

It was not uncommon to see a person, or maybe a small group of people, along a busy highway, thumb extended, hoping a motorist will be generous, stop, and give them a ride to their destination.

"That goes back to the hippy era, and it was just the way a lot of people got around," said Marv Balousek, the retired journalist. "I go back to the hippy era, and I know a lot of people traveled the country hitchhiking. I guess I did it a few times but not very much."

The 1970s was still a fairly innocent time. Most hitchhikers didn't think twice about jumping into a semi-truck driver's cab, or a middle-aged man's sedan. It's just a ride. What's the worst that could happen? Sure, you're taking a chance riding with a complete stranger, but most people are good, right?

Most people.

Henry Lee Lucas and Ottis Elwood Toole weren't like most people. A pair of deranged drifters, Lucas and Toole often took road trips in various parts of the U.S. in the '70s and early '80s. Most people trek cross country for sightseeing, relaxation, and new experiences.

Most people.

For Toole and Lucas, these excursions were hunting trips to find their next victim. They were on the hunt to abduct and kill.

The pair were known to make trips through Wisconsin. They were placed in Dane County on at least two occasions: 1976 and 1982. Debbie was murdered in the summer of '76.

After Toole was arrested in Florida in 1983, he told a detective from Menomonee Falls, Wisconsin that his partnership with Lucas led to "about a dozen" murders in Wisconsin. Lucas, after his arrest on a firearms violation in Texas, claimed the duo killed about 200 victims on their cross-country road trips.

"This statement is the truth as best as I can remember, and I think we killed somewhere around a dozen people in Wisconsin through the years, but I'd really have to sit down and think about it to get it straight where and when," Toole told Menomonee Falls police detective Jack Heitkemper.

At the time, Lucas and Toole were implicated in the murder of Joyce Gardner in 1981, a Menomonee Falls resident. Heitkemper told the *Capital Times* that Toole knew details about the Gardner homicide that only the killer would have known.

The homicide total would grow to three hundred. It ballooned to six hundred. Eventually, Lucas said he was involved in "thousands" of murders. Seem preposterous? That's because it is. In later years, it was determined Lucas was coerced into confessing to murders he didn't commit. However, Lucas, who died in 2001, was considered a serial killer. He's believed to have been linked to at least eleven murders, possibly as many as forty.

He had served time in prison for killing his mother in Michigan in 1960. In 1983, he was convicted of the murder of Frieda "Becky" Powell, believed to be his girlfriend. By January of 1984, Lucas had pleaded guilty to murdering a woman in her early eighties in Texas. Also at that time, he was ordered to stand trial for killing an unidentified woman hitchhiker, also in Texas.

Toole, meanwhile, had confessed to multiple murders, including killing young Adam Walsh in Hollywood, Florida in 1981. Walsh, six years old when he went missing, was the son of John Walsh, who started the popular TV series *America's Most Wanted* in the late 1980s. For many years, the weekly series profiled unsolved cases, identified wanted fugitives, and helped bring many runaway criminals to justice.

While Lucas and Toole's ties to Debbie's case were a long shot, detectives in Dane County had strong suspicions the pair was involved in Barbara Nelson's murder in 1982. Nelson, thirty-four, was abducted from a grocery store in Edgerton in August of that year. Two men attempted to rob the store, grabbed Nelson, and threw her into their truck.

Several days later, Nelson's body was discovered, shot and beaten, in a cornfield near Elkhorn, Wisconsin, about forty miles southeast from where she was abducted. As of 2022, the case has not been solved. Nelson's murder is one of two "unresolved" cases listed on the Dane County Sheriff's Office website, along with an armed robbery from 2011.

Not one of the seven cold cases profiled for this book are featured on the department's website under the unresolved cases tab.

Sketches of the two males who allegedly took Nelson were drawn on September 1, 1982 and filed with the sheriff's office. The sketches do not strike a resemblance to neither Lucas nor Toole.

Heitkemper interviewed Toole for two days in Florida. The detective came away with a good sense of the killer's psyche.

"You get no feeling of guilt. You get no feeling of right or wrong," he said in 1984. "You get no feeling of anything."

It's unclear if Toole and Lucas had a sexual relationship, but Heitkemper claimed Toole was gay. The detective also described the deranged thirty-six-year-old as a transvestite and a pyromaniac (he was serving twenty years in prison for arson in 1984). Besides being able to sign his name, Toole apparently couldn't read or write. He did have some street sense, Heitkemper claimed, at least more "than the average thief."

Toole told the detective most of the duo's victims lived

near freeways. Lucas would get lost if they strayed too far from a major highway. In Madison, Interstates 90 and 94 connect on the east side of the city. Interstate 90 runs north and south, while 94 goes east and west. Debbie's body was found a few miles southeast of Cross Plains, along a rural ditch, about twenty miles west of the I-90/94 connection point. That wouldn't align with Toole's statement about the pair sticking close to interstate highways.

But Debbie was last seen walking along Loftsgordon Avenue on the city's northeast side, roughly seven miles from the interstate connection. It's reasonable to think Lucas and Toole could have picked up Debbie, killed her, and traveled out of the city to get rid of the body and evidence. Since they had traveled through Wisconsin before, they likely had some familiarity with state and county highways.

While it could always remain a mystery whether Toole and Lucas killed Debbie, it wouldn't be the last time the pair would be suspected of murdering young women in the Madison area. Their names, especially Lucas,' would surface again. And, in the case of Julie Ann Hall, at least one Madison area detective was certain Lucas was his man.

CHAPTER 3

Julie Ann Hall, 1978

It had been a long week and Julie Hall was ready to go out, cut loose and have some fun.

Hall, who was nineteen at the time, had just gotten off of work at the Wisconsin State Historical Society in Madison. She had been working there for some time as an archivist. Julie enjoyed the work. She liked her co-workers. It was a good opportunity. A way for her to make some money, gain experience, and serve as a stepping-stone to something bigger. She was also looking to further her education.

But it was Friday night. She was young and single. It was time to party.

On the night of June 16, 1978, Julie met up with one of her brothers, Howard Hall, and a mutual friend, Jim Gunn. They decided to hit up the downtown bar scene near the state capitol for a fun night of drinking, sharing laughs, and catching up with friends. They were hoping to wind down the night smoking a little marijuana.

They began their night downing beers at the Main-

King Tap. The bar had a notorious reputation, closing its doors soon after Julie's murder. Howard eventually grew tired of the bar and wanted to venture out. He left Julie and Gunn at the Main King-Tap and went to hit up another establishment.

When Howard returned a while later, both Gunn and his sister were gone. Thinking she had found a way back to her apartment in Madison, her brother left and went home.

Not long after, Gunn also decided to make his way home. He and Julie parted ways at the corner of S. Pinckey Street and E. Main Street near the Capitol. He wasn't too worried about Julie. She seemed fine and was capable of finding a way back to her place.

"I didn't have a way to give her a ride home," Gunn said in a 2010 interview with NBC15 Madison. "As far as I can remember, she was going to go look for Howard."

Julie Ann Hall

Just before midnight on June 16 was the last time Gunn saw Julie Hall alive.

Five days later, on June 21, Julie's body was found partially buried in a shallow grave off Woodland Road, a few miles west of Waunakee, Wisconsin and about thirteen miles northwest of downtown Madison. She was found near a wooded farmland area, behind an old shed. Her nude body was left in what was thought to be a stump hole, hastily covered with dirt and leaves.

A farmer, walking along the area, noticed something strange about a pile of debris. It didn't look natural. He walked closer and received the shock of his life–a human foot sticking out of the brush pile.

Dane County Corner Clyde "Bud" Chamberlain believed Julie had been struck on the head with a blunt instrument. She could have also been sexually assaulted before she was murdered, for her body had many scratches on it. Did she put up a fight before she was killed? Or, were the scratches from her being dragged and placed in the shallow hole?

The Dane County Sheriff's Office, lead investigators on the case, told reporters no clues were left at the crime scene to indicate what was used to kill Julie.

Sheriff's office detectives interviewed both Howard Hall and Jim Gunn after her body was found. While investigators wouldn't provide many details about the conversations at the time, both men would later be cleared of any involvement in Julie's murder.

Her brother had stopped by the Historical Society the Tuesday after she went missing to see if Julie had been to work. She hadn't been there since the previous Friday. Julie's absence struck her supervisor as odd. Julie always made it to work on time every day.

He came in again on Thursday just to check. There was a report about a body being found. He didn't want to believe it was Julie, his only sister, but when dental records confirmed the following day it was her, the crushing weight of reality sunk in.

Julie's supervisor, who was interviewed by the *Capital Times* but did not disclose her name, said news of her death sent a ripple of shock and horror through her body. "Death like this usually doesn't strike so close," she said.

Julie began working at the Historical Society on May 1. While she had only been there for several weeks, co-workers and managers got to know her. She was friendly, outgoing, trusting, and happy. Julie came to work with a smile on her face. She was open and sincere.

"She was close to her family," said the supervisor. "She was always talking about her brothers."

And there were plenty of brothers to talk about. In a family of eight, Julie was the only sister. The Halls grew up in Fennimore, Wisconsin, about seventy miles directly west of Madison. Julie graduated from Southwest Wisconsin Vocational Institute (known today as Southwest Wisconsin Technical College), before moving to Madison.

Hardworking and ambitious, Julie was filled with dreams and aspirations.

"She knew she was going to do something," her brother Mike Hall said in 2010. "And she was going for it."

Her parents, Betty and Donne, divorced in 1977. Betty relocated to Baraboo, Wisconsin, (Julie lived with her for a time before moving to Madison), while Donne stayed in Fennimore. Whether money drove a wedge between the couple is unclear, but the Halls won $300,000 in the Illinois State Lottery in 1975. Two years later, they were separated and living in other parts of the state.

Motive Clear, But Who Did It?

For the months and years following Julie's murder, her case mostly grew cold.

No suspects were publicly announced, and it didn't appear investigators were close to making any arrests. In the spring of 1981, however, a story in the State *Journal* shed new light on Julie's case.

George Hesselberg, serving as the paper's police reporter in the early '80s, reported that police were close to cracking the Hall case, they were just "waiting for a break." By May of 1981, Steve Urso, a Dane County Sheriff's Office deputy, had been working on the Hall case for nearly three years. The weight of being tasked with trying to solve Julie's case, along with other high-profile unsolved murders, left Urso haggard but determined to forge ahead.

"All I can say is there is no statute of limitations on murder," Urso told the State *Journal*.

Urso, along with help from Madison detectives Mary Ostrander and Ted Mell, believed they had pinpointed a strong motive in Julie's murder: sex.

"But we don't have the cause of death, we don't have the evidence, and we certainly don't have a confession," Urso said.

Detectives felt they knew who killed the young woman and why she was murdered. In fact, Urso was "confident" police had the correct suspect lined up.

Since there was little evidence to work with it was difficult for police to piece together a theory of how Julie was killed. They believed she was sexually assaulted before she was bashed over the head. Her body was found with scratch marks on it, suggesting Julie fought with her attacker before receiving the fatal blow.

Autopsy and toxicology results in the 1970s weren't as advanced as they are now, but based on what police knew about her death, another interesting theory emerged. Perhaps Julie was still alive when her killer crudely buried her with brush in that hollowed-out stump hole. Perhaps she never regained consciousness and died after hours of being exposed to the elements.

The thought that Julie's fragile life could have been saved if the killer would have had a change of heart, gone back, picked her out of the brush pile, and taken her to a hospital is nauseating. But then, someone with the type of deranged mind to commit such a violent act likely doesn't think in those terms. They probably thought Julie was already dead. Leaving her like they did—nude, concealed by brush in a shallow, wooded area—was a near perfect way to conceal the body and destroy evidence.

In 1982, the shocking murder of Paula McCormick, a ten-year-old girl, gripped Madison and sent chills across Wisconsin. Roger Lange, a twenty-seven-year-old man, was convicted of kidnapping and killing Paula. Lange was known to frequent bars along the Capitol Square. He also had a negative reputation with downtown Madison patrol officers.

After Lange confessed to murdering Paula, there was speculation he could be connected to the murders of other young women, but he was never formally named a suspect.

As more time passed, and no arrests were made, police continued to consider other suspects. Maybe the person who killed Julie was a suspect in other Madison area cases. Maybe he struck less than two years earlier when Debra Bennett became a victim of homicide.

Lucas Grilled by Detectives

In the spring of 1984, several investigators from three Wisconsin jurisdictions traveled to Texas, eager to interview a man suspected of murdering more than a hundred victims.

Henry Lee Lucas, awaiting trial for a murder in Texas, claimed to have killed more than a hundred and sixty-five people with accomplice, Ottis Elwood Toole. However, as mentioned previously, authorities couldn't trust much of what Lucas was telling them. Yes, he was known to be a violent murderer, but his claims seemed to be preposterous.

Detectives from Dane County, the city of Madison and Walworth County, Wisconsin, however, had a strong belief Lucas was involved with at least a few of the state's unsolved murders. Dane County Sheriff Jerome Lacke especially felt Lucas was a prime suspect in the Debra Bennett case, but could he have also killed Julie Hall?

State Journal police reporter Marv Balousek interviewed Lacke a few months before local detectives traveled south to interview the suspected serial killer.

"It definitely appears he was in the vicinity of at least one (if not more) of the homicide cases we're working on with female victims," Lacke said in the news story. "It would be irresponsible not to interview him and try to refresh his memory."

Lacke believed Lucas was in the Madison area in 1976

when Bennett was murdered, but had not confirmed he was in Wisconsin in 1978 when Hall was killed. Still, police had to consider him a suspect.

"They sent a team of detectives down there, (to Texas where Lucas was in prison), one I believe was from Fort Atkinson (Wisconsin) because there had been a murder over there of a young couple, so they were checking on that," Balousek said. "He was convicted of murder, so was a murderer, there was no question about that."

The questioning of Lucas, originally scheduled for mid-March, was pushed back to mid-June. For local detectives, it was a frustrating waiting game, but it allowed them more time to prepare. And, once they sat down with Lucas, the experience was like nothing they've ever been through before.

The June 15, 1984 edition of the *Capital Times* ran a photo of Lucas that provided a window into his delusional mind. A year earlier, the *Associated Press* snapped a photo of Lucas, sporting a wide and mostly toothless grin. He had partially unbuttoned his prison uniform to show a black T-shirt underneath, emblazoned with the word "Jesus" across the chest. Cigarette dangling from one hand, he was proud to show off his new calling in life. Miraculously, after being arrested in 1983 and suspected of multiple homicides, Lucas had found Jesus. He was suddenly a born-again Christian.

In the following day's edition, *Capital Times*' staff writer Sharon D. Pitman succinctly set the scene of how the nine-hour marathon interview with Lucas began.

Henry Lee Lucas leaned back in a chair at a Texas

prison early this week and told how he killed and mutilated one of his more than three hundred victims. He then sat up, took a bite from a hamburger on the table in front of him, sipped from a cup of coffee, and continued the tales of horror.

While they had to make an effort to get valuable information from Lucas, Madison area police knew he would never stand trial in Wisconsin, even if he confessed to some of the unsolved murders. Lucas was already serving a death sentence for being convicted of four murders in Texas. Madison Police Chief David Couper, however, felt obligated to the friends and families of Debra Bennett, Julie Hall, and other victims such as Julie Speerschneider, Shirley Stewart, and Susan LeMahieu. If Lucas was connected to even one of the murders, it would bring a sense of closure to a local family.

"We owe it to the families of the victims so that they'll know what happened," Couper said.

Couper told the press he was about "eighty percent sure" Lucas was responsible for at least one of the murders involving young women in Madison. He would not go on the record which victim it was, citing his desire to first talk to family members.

While Couper thought follow-up interviews with Lucas were likely needed to pull more information, the police chief believed detectives had enough from the first interrogation to "see whether or not he is telling the truth."

David Cochems, a detective with the Dane County Sheriff's Office, had a sinking feeling Lucas killed Hall after grilling him in that Texas prison. Lucas knew too much about the case not to be involved, Cochems thought.

"When I got down to specifics, he walked me through it," Cochems told Pitman. "I knew he was there."

After Lucas was convicted of the four murders in Texas, more information came out about his troubled upbringing. He was the youngest of thirteen children. His father, having lost both legs in a railroad accident, drank excessively and his mother, a known sex worker, was abusive. Lucas stabbed his mother to death in 1960. He claimed it was self-defense after she had attacked him with a broom stick, but Lucas was still sentenced to fifteen years in prison. He was released in the summer of 1975.

In the 1984 interview with police, Lucas came off as cool and collected. He was void of any emotion.

"He will give you specific answers to specific questions or in general about murdering women and show no remorse," Cochems said.

In a June 17 story about the Lucas interviews, Balousek wrote:

> *Investigators say Lucas has an almost detached view of his crimes, often puffing calmly on a cigarette while he discussed brutality and torture.*

Cochems, a seasoned detective by 1984, felt queasy face-to-face with Lucas.

"My skin crawled and my nerves were on edge," he said.

Herb Hanson, from the UW Police Department (then

known as University Police and Security), was one of three detectives, along with Cochems and Mary Otterson from the Madison Police Department, to interview Lucas in Georgetown, Texas. When contacted for an interview in 2021, the elderly Hanson declined to say much about his experience meeting the deranged Lucas.

"I sit in the shadows and reflect," Hanson said. "At this point, I am not a public information source!"

One couldn't blame Hanson for trying to forget an encounter with Lucas. Yet, Lucas was considered charming and relatable. Coachems said he had "an ability to talk to people." That's likely how he was able to lure victims into his vehicle. Young women saw him as disarming, friendly, and engaging.

Lucas possessed that aura when discussing his gruesome crimes to detectives. In one segment of the interview, he claimed he stabbed a Texas school teacher twenty-six times. Whether he was making it up or not, Lucas described the brutality in such detail he had investigators convinced he was there.

"There are some things so terrible that you can't forget them," he told the police.

Lucas was also very manipulative, which worked to his advantage when he was traveling the country, spotting his next victim. A lonely, desperate female hitchhiker probably welcomed Lucas' kind demeanor.

Was he cunning enough to fool veteran investigators with years of interrogation experience?

"Some of these guys are really manipulative. I don't know whether he's manipulating them or not but maybe he followed the questioning to where they were leading them," Balousek said. "'Was the body left behind the bush? 'Yeah, I think the body was left behind the bush.' He could have manipulated them into thinking he did this, but these were seasoned detectives, and they knew their business, knew their job, and he convinced them he did this."

At the time of the June 1984 interviews with Madison area police, Lucas had been charged with twenty murders. In twisted descriptiveness, Lucas bragged that he killed in nearly every conceivable way. He also burned bodies. Debra Bennett's body was burned.

"I've killed them most every way but poison," Lucas said.

How mentally unhinged does a person have to be to commit even a handful of murders? Balousek reported that while Lucas did serve some prison time after killing his mother, most of it was spent in a mental hospital. Toole, considered psychologically unstable himself, hooked up with Lucas after the former was released from prison in 1975.

After being arrested for a gun charge in 1983, Lucas began his numerous tales of confessions. While in custody in Texas, Lucas passed a note to a guard that read: "I've done something terrible." He then confessed to killing eighty-two-year-old Kate Rich in Ringgold, Texas.

Lucas was later sentenced to death for strangling and killing a hitchhiker in 1979. His other convictions carried two life sentences and a seventy-five-year sentence for another murder.

It was also suggested in local press accounts that Lucas and Toole were "lovers." Lucas said he had family in Superior, Wisconsin and often traveled up there via the interstate from Milwaukee. Richard Wellner, a Jefferson County (Wisconsin) detective who also interviewed Lucas, said he and Toole "traveled the interstate highways and they usually got rid of their victims in secluded places and killed them at random."

Lucas claimed victims all across Wisconsin and northeastern Minnesota. He admitted to murders in Milwaukee, West Bend, rural areas west of Plymouth, and south of Manitowoc, Wisconsin. While visiting relatives in Superior, Lucas, as he put it, managed to find time to sneak away and kill near Duluth, Minnesota.

Toole, meanwhile, was the main suspect in the May 1981 murder of Menomonee Falls resident Joyce Garder. After local detectives quizzed Toole in July, a month after questioning Lucas, they determined Toole was not involved in the murders of several Madison women, including Julie Hall. By early August, the Dane County Sheriff's Office was preparing cases against Lucas to be forwarded to the county's district attorney.

Investigators were truly bewildered by Lucas. At times, he gave very specific details about alleged murders he committed. Other times, his claims of murder were far-fetched. He told Wellner he murdered a victim near Palmyra, Wisconsin in 1978. He said he abducted the victim from a Hardee's restaurant, of which there was none.

"There were other things that didn't match," Wellner told the *State Journal*. "He probably killed someone the way he described, but not in Palmyra."

Still, Lucas had to be considered for a few of the Madison area murders. He was believable ... to a point.

"Before my interview with him, I sat in while Lucas

was being interviewed by another Wisconsin detective and was astonished by the details he gave to that killing," Wellner said. "He told only things the killer would know. After that I believed he committed the murders he admitted. I still question the number, however."

Wellner had also interviewed Toole. The detective thought Lucas was more trustworthy than the "incredibly stupid" Toole. Wellner said Toole spun tales of drinking human blood and eating body parts. For a pair of sick individuals, Wellner described Toole as more disgusting than Lucas.

"Lucas was very cool and matter-of-fact about his crimes," said Wellner. "It was enough to spook you. I won't forget it for some time to come."

After the interviews with Lucas, Balousek wrote a news analysis piece headlined "Killers may represent a new breed of murderer" for the *State Journal*. Balousek suggested murderers such as Lucas, who were known to abduct or pick up their victims as hitchhikers, "represent a new phenomenon of highly mobile murderers, leaving behind strings of slayings without a clear motive."

Balousek reported that between 1981 and 1983, the total number of murders across the U.S. fell by six percent. Motiveless slayings, however, increased by about three percent. In the demented minds of Lucas and Toole, their victims died for no rhyme or reason.

"Why he confessed and then recanted, I don't know. Maybe he wanted the publicity. Maybe he wanted trips around the country, because they did take him to see (potential crime scenes)," Balousek said. "Otis Toole had been convicted of killing John Walsh's son, abducted, and killed. So, they didn't discriminate in who they killed, this was just a young child, just unbelievable. I don't think they interviewed Toole as much in connection to these murders, I think Lucas was more their guy. Toole wasn't a major factor in it. He wasn't a very bright guy either so probably couldn't be as manipulative.

They had traveled through Wisconsin around the times of those murders, so that's why they believed it. So maybe it was true, but then he recanted so much. Plus, they didn't have evidence, they just had his confession, that's all they had."

Case Re-examination Provides Hope

In 2010, Dane County Detectives Mary Butler and Dawn Johnson took a fresh look at the Julie Hall cold case. They believed they were close to a breakthrough.

"We truly feel this case is solvable," Butler said.

In an effort to spark renewed public interest in the case, the detectives–with the cooperation of family members–did an interview with Madison TV station NBC15 in November of 2010.

Butler, hoping to find any shred of forensic evidence she could, returned to the spot Julie's body was found. At that point, more than three decades had passed since the murder and the site's topography had certainly changed since the summer of 1978. The seasoned detective did, however, find enough evidence to submit it to the Wisconsin State Crime Lab for DNA testing.

"Some was recovered on her, and some was recovered elsewhere," Butler said.

In the weeks following the homicide, investigators determined Julie had consumed a large meal before she was attacked. Detectives believed sometime in the early morning hours, Julie ate at a restaurant between Madison and Waunakee. Police were hoping for witnesses to come forward saying they saw the nineteen-year-old dining out that night. Nobody did.

"Published appeals for information haven't brought a single call, according to investigators," reported the *Capital Times* on June 29, 1978.

When Johnson and Butler re-examined the case years later, the more they looked at the circumstances, the more they felt whoever killed Julie knew her. After not finding Howard, Julie might have run into someone she knew. Being young, trusting, and a little naïve, Julie could have accepted a ride from this person. Hungry from a long night of drinking, they stopped to grab a bite to eat.

After dinner, something went terribly wrong.

Perhaps someone tried to make a move on Julie, she pushed him away and he grew angry from rejection. A jolted person could have snapped and in a fit of rage, struck Julie over the head, killing her. Johnson said the fact Julie's body was found behind a structure covered with brush and dirt shows she wasn't simply discarded.

"She was hidden from view, which leads me to believe that person knew her," Johnson told NBC15. "That's why they hid her, they were buying time."

The night she disappeared, Julie was wearing a shirt, bib overalls or jeans, a bandana, moccasins, and plastic, brown-framed glasses. She was found nude, and her clothing was never recovered.

During the TV interview, Johnson all but pleaded for someone to come forward with information. More than a decade later, the case remains open.

"Sometimes people think they don't need to come forward because somebody else is going to," Johnson said. "Please don't do that. Please come forward yourself."

He didn't directly come out and say it in the interview, but it appeared Mike Hall also believed the killer knew Julie. After decades of no answers, the Hall family was putting out a call to action.

"It's time for everybody to step up," Mike said. "That's why it's so hard to accept."

Despite being questioned by detectives and cleared of any wrongdoing, both Gunn and Howard Hall were viewed with an eye of suspicion. Friends thought they had to have known more. They were the last people to see Julie alive that night in 1978.

For Gunn, grieving Julie's shocking murder was difficult with even people close to him doubting his innocence.

"We (Howard and I) both know that neither one of us did it," Gunn said in 2010.

Through the years, Gunn and Howard Hall drifted apart like many young friends eventually do. But they remained on good terms and kept in touch from time to time.

"We don't hang around together a lot, but I still talk to him," Gunn said.

By 2010, Betty Hall was elderly and needed in-home care. Mike Hall, one her eight children, was caring for her at the time of the NBC15 interview. Betty had lost a child in a horrific, violent fashion. Thirty-two years had passed since her daughter's life was brutally cut short, but a mother's grief and loss were still painfully etched across Betty's face.

"I can't help to think ... well, she would have kids by now ... and I would have grandkids."

Betty died a few years later never knowing who killed her only daughter.

CHAPTER 4

Julie Speerschneider, 1979

Julie Speerschneider was walking along Johnson Street, one block from her friend's house when she vanished.

It was March 27, 1979. A cold, foggy night. Julie, a twenty-year-old Madison resident, had just hitched a ride to Johnson and figured she could just walk the short distance to her friend's place. She had had fun tonight at the 602 Club near the UW-Madison campus, but it was nearing 9:00 p.m. It was a Tuesday night and she had to work the next morning.

Despite not attending college, she was the age of most college students. She enjoyed going out and having a good time, just like them. Unlike many students at UW, however, Julie was juggling three jobs. She had already started life at a time most women her age was still trying to figure life out.

Julie was ready to wind down. She was excited to see her friend, catch up a little, and watch a movie. Probably call it a night after that. Get ready for another day.

Get ready for another day...

Julie never showed up at her friend's house. The friend thought it was strange, since she had just talked to Julie. She had called her around 8:30 p.m. from the Memorial Union on campus.

"I'll be there right away," Julie replied.

But perhaps she had hitched a ride back home. It wouldn't have been a big surprise. Julie was known to hitch rides around Madison, especially along Johnson Street.

Then Wednesday arrived. No Julie. Thursday came and went. No Julie. She had not shown up for the past three days at either of her jobs, at Tony's Chop Suey restaurant, the Red Caboose Day Care Center, or the daycare on Baldwin Street. Since it had been more than forty-eight hours since anyone last saw her, she officially became a missing person.

On March 31, a small brief, headlined: "20-Year-Old Woman Reported Missing," ran in the *Capital Times*. The three-paragraph article printed two numbers to call for anyone who knew anything about Julie's disappearance. Her family offered a $500 reward for information.

The following day, the *State Journal* also ran a report on Julie with a bit more information. The paper ran a headshot photo of her. Julie had long brown hair, a soft, innocent smile, and friendly, welcoming eyes. The night she disappeared Julie was wearing blue jeans, boots, and a blue and gray-striped Mexican poncho. Julie was slightly underdressed considering it was only in the upper twenties with overcast skies when she left the bar to call her friend. Unseasonably cold for Madison in late March, but definitely not shocking early "spring" weather in Wisconsin.

Julie Speerschneider

Days passed. Weeks passed. Still no Julie.

By mid-May, after nearly two months since anyone last saw Julie, her family and friends started a search fund. The goal was to raise $8,000 by June 1 to hire a private investigator to search for their loved one. They also wanted to increase the $500 reward for information to her whereabouts.

On May 16, friends held a press conference announcing the fund at the Wil-Mar Neighborhood Center, 953 Jenifer Street, Madison. The announcement wasn't far from where Julie lived with friends Gail Greenberg and Gary Rizzo at 524 S. Dickinson St. on the city's East Side. Her friends asked the public to chip in what they could to the "Community Search for Julie," set up through the First Federal Savings and Loan Association on State Street in Madison.

By May, police had pieced together some clues in Julie's case. She hitchhiked a ride with a tall, young man. Investigators wanted to find that man.

Friends and family didn't believe Julie simply up and left. That wasn't like her. Not on her own, at least. Julie was not known to take trips without telling family and friends first.

On the night she went missing, Julie didn't have a purse with her. She carried no identification. No money had been taken from her bank account in the weeks after she left. No clothing or other personal items were taken from her room at the house on Dickinson. She had three jobs and while it was difficult at times to balance everything, she had never missed work.

"We are convinced that Julie has not walked off on her own," her mother, Joan, said at the press conference.

If she had decided to run off with someone, she did a poor job of preparing for it.

The hitchhiking. Her mom was not pleased her daughter often accepted rides from strangers, but she understood why. Julie's car had broken down earlier in the year. She had yet to find a replacement and depended on others to give her a lift.

Almost two months had passed with no leads. For Joan and David, Julie's father, the feeling of not knowing tormented the Speerschneider's every day. While local police pursued the case, the couple looked into other ways to find information on Julie. They talked to two psychics.

People can often be skeptical of the value of psychics. Do they really have the power to see what others don't? Are they really well-intentioned, hoping to help people, or are they out to exploit? Prey on a vulnerable person's emotions to make a few quick bucks?

By the spring of 1979, however, the Speerschneiders were desperate for any leads. Any piece of information. Any point of direction that could break open the case.

While that could mean hearing something the family didn't want to hear, it was worth a shot.

Psychics told Julie's parents their daughter was dead. They would find her body buried, about thirteen miles northeast of Madison in the town of Burke. Detectives from Dane County and the city of Madison searched the area. Friends joined in the search. They found nothing. It was another frustrating day for all involved, but ... were the psychics on to something? Julie's mother believed they were.

"It looks that way," Joan Speerschneider told reporters when asked if she believed the psychics premonitions.

Madison detective Mary Ostrander, also still working on the Julie Hall case, was the lead investigator on the Speerschneider case. Ostrander, a hard-driving, dedicated cop, was trying to pursue every lead she could, but there was little to go on.

Jack Smith, another friend of Julie's, wasn't so fond of the police's work on the case. "We have to work on the leads we have," Smith was told. He thought police weren't being aggressive enough in tracking down new information.

"We have genuine respect for law enforcement agencies," Smith said. "But there is a serious flaw in the system that depends upon passive investigation."

Smith said the public could have a hand in solving his friend's case. They could support the fund or help search for Julie.

Police did find a man that said he thought he had picked up Julie and gave her ride on March 27. He said he drove Julie and another man to Johnson Street and let them out a block from her friend's house. Did anyone see anything unusual? Did another motorist stop and offer Julie a ride after she had been let out?

"Someone knows what happened that night," Joan Speerschneider said.

Through fundraising efforts, Julie's friends and family were hoping to hire Sandra Sutherland, a private investigator from San Francisco. Sutherland led a P.I. agency in the Bay Area. She had a strong reputation. A Madison attorney told Julie's friends Sutherland would be a good person to take on the case. She had an excellent track record in solving missing person cases, but she wouldn't come cheap.

Julie was clearly loved by a lot of caring people. There was no question she was missed. Among her roommates, Rizzo and Greenberg, other friends spearheading the drive were Bridget Farrelly, Sherry Martin, Renee Grisman, Patty Lew, and Judy Rybrecki.

Police Turn to Hypnosis

Running out of options and with Julie still missing after several weeks, local police turned to an unconventional method—hypnosis.

It may have been a last-ditch effort to find a lead, but detectives were determined to try. They felt hypnosis could be used on witnesses to unlock a crucial piece of evidence in the case. While the technique wasn't common in Madison or Dane County policing, at least back in the '70s, hypnosis can be used to help a witness recall certain events in detail. In some areas of the U.S., it was a common practice, especially for victims of violent crime. By tapping into the subconscious mind, victims can sometimes recall terrible events they've blocked out through "going under."

Hypnosis can also be a flawed technique and not a credible procedure to solve crimes. Local police weren't seriously thinking about using hypnosis on a regular basis, but in the Speerschneider case, they were downright desperate.

"There are times when we have cases with few leads and we have to use extraordinary methods," Jack Heibel, detective captain for the Madison Police Department, told the *Capital Times*.

Investigators were hopeful they caught a break when they found the man who gave Julie a ride to Johnson Street. More like he found them. After learning about the missing twenty-year-old, he contacted police and said he would like to help.

However, the young man's memory was foggy. Several weeks had passed and he couldn't recall for certain the young woman was Julie. He agreed to answer questions through hypnosis.

Through the help of Dr. Roger Severson, a clinical psychologist and UW-Madison professor, the man was put under hypnosis. Throughout the session, Detective Ostrander carefully probed the man with questions. Like a portal into the mind's past, the trance brought him back to that night in Madison.

He remembered picking Julie up on the corner of Johnson and State Street. She was wearing a Mexican poncho. He also recalled another man hitching a ride. Small talk was made on the short drive. Julie didn't appear to know the other passenger. The driver let them both out at the corner of Johnson and Brearly Street. They apparently walked away in opposite directions; Julie walked up Brearly and the man crossed Johnson.

To the man who gave Julie a lift, the pretty young woman with long brown hair and an easy-going smile was a fleeting memory. A brief interaction in a busy life of hundreds of interactions. Meeting Julie was a small moment in his life; no wonder the images were a bit hazy.

For Julie's friends and family, however, who knew her well and loved spending time with her, Julie would never be forgotten.

On July 27, 1979, four months to the day Julie vanished, the Madison Theater Guild put on a production of "The Fantastics." It was held at 8:00 p.m. at the McDaniels Auditorium inside the School Administration Building at 545 W. Dayton St. Proceeds from the play would go to the fund to help find Julie Speerschneider.

Months of detective work, fifteen psychics, hypnosis, a high-priced private investigator, and the never-ending efforts of those close to Julie, was still not enough. The case grew colder by the day.

Body Found Near River

Charles Byrd decided to go for a walk on the afternoon of April 18, 1981.

It was nice out, seasonable with temperatures hovering around sixty degrees. Byrd walked along the Yahara River, just north of Lake Kegonsa. The lake, part of a chain of four lakes in the Madison area, is southeast of the capital city, near McFarland. As the day crept along, clouds filled the mid-April sky. Rain wasn't in the forecast, so Byrd didn't think he would get caught in a downpour.

Byrd strolled through a thicket of woods that hugged the banks of the Yahara. For a sixteen-year-old kid, it was a nice way to kill time on a lazy Saturday. After months of the winter doldrums, it was finally spring in Wisconsin. Chores, homework, whatever awaited him back home could wait another day. It was a bit breezy, but hey, a fine sixty-degree day in April was nothing to scoff at. And, this was a secluded area. Not many people walk down here. For a curious teenager, it was fun to explore.

As he approached the river, Byrd noticed something strange. It was barely visible but something was definitely there. Could it be? No. It was. A skeleton was lying in the woods near the riverbank. Was it a deer? That's certainly possible. But as Byrd carefully walked up to the remains, his heart sank. This was definitely not an animal.

~

By Monday afternoon, it was confirmed. The gruesome discovery Byrd had made over the weekend was the remains of Julie Speerschneider.

Dr. Richard C. Buescher, Julie's dentist, matched her dental records to the body. However, more than two years had passed since she went missing. With the state her body was in, it was nearly impossible to determine exactly how she died.

Chamberlain, the county coroner, said there was no clothing found on Julie's body or near the site where she was found. The only clue? A single braid of brown hair tied together with a decorative elastic band.

Julie's body was placed face down. It was covered by twigs and branches. Was it an attempt to hide the body?

It was placed there "like it was put there intentionally and covered up," said Deputy Coroner Donald Scullion.

Based on published reports, Byrd found her body about fifty feet from the riverbank and around forty feet from Yahara Drive, a short gravel road with access to cottages along the Yahara. Considering there's only a slice of woods between the gravel road and the river, it's somewhat amazing nobody found the body prior to April of 1981. Was it really laying there for two years? That's assuming the killer didn't move the body from another location and place it near the riverbank.

By the spring of '81, Mary Ostrander had a bulging two-inch-thick folder on the Speerschneider case staring back at her on her desk. The Madison detective had devoted months to working on Julie's missing person case. She was hoping to find her alive. Now Ostrander was tasked to find her killer.

"This is the most frustrating case I've ever worked on," an exasperated Ostrander told the local press.

Ironically, and somewhat ominously, it was Ostrander who eerily predicted how Julie's body would be found. Several psychics claimed she was killed, and her body was placed in a wooded area near a body of water. Police searched locations around Dane County and Adams County, a rural area north of Wisconsin Dells, that matched the psychics' descriptions, but to no avail.

Less than a month prior to Byrd's discovery, Ostrander was interviewed by local media. Two years had passed since Julie went missing. There wasn't much new to report on the case. It frustrated the seasoned detective to no end. But Ostrander wanted the public—especially Julie's loved ones—to know that she was doing everything in her power to crack the case.

"If she is found, it will be some hunter who stumbled across her body in the woods somewhere," Ostrander said.

The spot where Julie's body was found was described as an "out-of-the-way area." Perhaps her killer knew the area well, knowing it was a location people seldom touched.

While two years had passed since Julie's disappearance, and hope she would be found alive deteriorated as months turned into years, the discovery of her remains was still shocking. Friends who circulated missing person posters across Madison had a difficult time coping with the reality that Julie was gone and likely murdered.

Also, since Julie juggled multiple jobs, her death left a void with co-workers and bosses. They missed her warm personality and dedicated work ethic. Along with her daycare work, Julie also logged hours at Tony's Chop Suey Restaurant, 616 S. Park St., near the UW campus.

Anthony Wong, who owned Tony's, told the *State Journal*, "She was a really good worker, a good employee."

Julie only spent a few months at the restaurant, but she had a lasting impression on the staff and customers.

"She was a very nice person to work with," a fellow co-worker recalled.

After reports circulated that a body was found southeast of McFarland, Scullion fielded calls from anxious, anguished parents and friends. They too had missing daughters, girlfriends, sisters, and roommates. Here one day, gone the next. Still out there. Somewhere.

They dialed Scullion's number, praying it wasn't their missing loved one.

"The parents I called and told it wasn't their daughter were very grateful," the detective told the *State Journal.* "This is rough on parents."

On one hand, finding a body—devasting as it is—brings a small sense of closure to victims' families and friends. On the other hand, not finding the person deceased presents a crack of daylight. It's a tiny slice of hope they're still out there, alive.

For the Speerschneider family, however, their worst fears were realized. Psychics had predicted Julie was killed nearly two years earlier. They said she would be found near a body of water, in or near a wooded lot. While the exact location was off, it's eerie to think how right they were.

On May 7, criminal pathologist Dr. Billy Bauman came back with Julie's cause of death: undetermined. It made sense considering only skeletal remains were found. And, this was 1981. Forensic science wasn't as advanced as it is today.

Bauman's determination mattered little to investigators. Julie Speerschneider was murdered. The case has been treated as a homicide for more than forty years.

To help with the investigation, police sent a photo of a similar-looking sarape or Mexican poncho Julie was wearing the night she disappeared to local media. It was a longshot, but someone might have seen her wearing the poncho, along with whoever picked her up, on that dreary March night in 1979.

"Anyone with possible information about this sarape, or who may have seen her that evening, is asked to call Madison police detectives at 266-4945," read part of the photo caption.

Detectives Go Back to Lucas

"Raping, robbing, and stealing."

That's what allegedly preoccupied Henry Lee Lucas' life on his trips to Wisconsin in the late 1970s and early 1980s. In May of '84, Lucas told a detective from Milwaukee that he drove up to Wisconsin six or seven times between '79 and '82.

Lucas claimed to have killed eight victims during his time in Wisconsin, including one in Madison.

"However, the details he provided of the Madison killing did not fit any unsolved cases," wrote Balousek in the *State Journal.*

So, it made sense, as the years rolled by and the Speerschneider case remained cold, that police would consider Lucas a possible suspect.

Lucas, already convicted of multiple murders, had been a suspect in the Julie Hall homicide. Hall's body was found in June of 1978. Less than a year later, Speerschneider went missing. Lucas had bragged about killing "hundreds" of victims, but when Madison detectives interviewed him for the Speerscheider case in 1984, little did they know that many of his "confessions" would turn out to be total fabrications.

Lucas, along with his murdering partner, Ottis Toole, tended to pursue young women with troubled backgrounds. Speerschneider, ambitious, hard-working with multiple jobs and a loving group of family and friends, didn't seem to fit the mold. But the pair were known to pick up hitchhikers. Julie had a penchant for hitchhiking.

"Someone must have abducted her or something," Balousek said in a 2021 interview. "Whoever it was was apparently really good at covering their tracks."

Interviewed through Zoom, Balousek thinks at least some of the murders from the late '70s and early '80s–especially Debra Bennett, Julie Hall, Julie Speerscheider, Susan Lemahieu, and Shirley Stewart–are all linked to the same killer.

"I tend to think it was the same killer, of those women in the middle, because the cases were so similar," Balousek said, referring to the point that all of the bodies were found in wooded areas.

Three detectives, David Cochems from the Dane County Sheriff's Office, Herb Hanson of the UW police, and Ted Mell from the Madison Police Department, traveled to Georgetown, Texas in early June of '84 to grill Lucas.

Several weeks passed before local police decided it was time to release their findings from the Lucas interview. And it was a stunner.

"Mass killer blamed for city murder," was the headline splashed across the front page of the Saturday, August 4 edition of the *State Journal.*

Investigators were convinced Lucas murdered Julie Speerschneider. Detectives claimed Lucas told them specific details of the murder only the killer would know. Dane County Sheriff Jerome Lacke, in speaking to the press, wouldn't go beyond the basics of the investigators' report, but it was still a shocking revelation.

It's possible Lucas could have read news reports about the case in the years leading up to the interview. Without knowing exactly what Lucas said in that Texas prison, it's difficult to determine how accurate he was. Hanson, one of the three detectives who quizzed Lucas, declined to be interviewed about the Speerschneider case when contacted in 2021.

Lucas was cooperative and calm during the interviews. While his answers may have seemed rock solid, he was known to be very manipulative. Its possible investigators were fooled by his charm and laid-back demeanor.

In September 1984, Lucas took a trip to California. He took detectives to sites where he claimed to have killed several victims. As a result, police believed they had solved fifteen murders.

~

On October 7, 1983, Detective Mary Ostrander turned in her badge.

The veteran Madison police officer was retiring after twenty-five years on the force. Ostrander had solved many crimes and helped countless city residents through the years. One unsolved case still mystified her, however, even as she was ready to leave law enforcement behind.

"I turned over the Julie Speerschneider file this morning," Ostrander told George Hesselberg of the *State Journal.*

After more than four years of exhaustively investigating every lead possible, Ostrander couldn't make an arrest. It wouldn't be her case to worry about anymore, but it would still keep Ostrander up at night, years after she left the Madison police.

"I think we know who did it, but we can't prove it," Ostrander said. "It's the one case I really did things I have never done before."

Steve Urso, another Madison detective who had worked on the case, retired shortly before Ostrander. Urso also believed they were close to nailing the person responsible for her death. They just failed to land that smoking gun.

"It can be one of two people," Urso told the *State Journal.*

On Sunday, September 8, 1994, Mary Ostrander died. She was only sixty years old.

Ostrander had battled diabetes and kidney failure. She had been very ill since the winter of 1993. Her body decided it was time to stop fighting.

By the early 1990s, Hesselberg had been promoted to a columnist slot at the *State Journal.* He wrote a lot about people who had died. He penned a touching tribute to Ostrander, sharing how the veteran cop was steadfast in her fight to hire and promote more women on the Madison police force.

Her final case was the Speerschneider homicide.

"Ostrander shared the assignment on that case, and it

bothered her mightily that it wasn't cracked," Hesselberg wrote in his column.

It's been almost three decades since Ostrander passed away and justice still waits for Julie Speerschneider.

Case Reopened Decades Later

After heavy investigation and suspicion of Lucas died down by the mid-1980s (he was never convicted of murdering Julie Speerschneider), the case file was closed and mostly sat dormant for about thirty years.

In the mid-2010s, however, the file was dusted off and a new generation of detectives got a fresh look at Julie's murder.

Through a state-funded grant, Madison police had a three-year period to work on unsolved cases. Detective Dan Nale, who served as a detective from 2008-2018, was one of the investigators assigned to the cold case unit. Nale wasn't sure why the Speerschneider case was targeted for re-investigation, but he was eager to jump into it.

Nale spent a few hours a week digging through files, pouring through old cases. For almost a year, from September 2015 to May 2016, Nale worked on the Speerschneider case.

"That was about what the grant was able to deal with as far as officer overtime," Nale said. "A lot of times the (overtime) would come in the beginning from just reading the case."

When reached for a phone interview in 2021, Nale was open and straightforward, but couldn't provide concrete details on what investigators discovered when they reopened the Speerschneider case.

"I can't give you specifics because it is still an open case but what I can tell you is we went over it with a fine-toothed comb," Nale said. "The cold case unit had representatives from our forensics unit on it."

Since the cold case team only had about three years to use the state grant, investigators tried to make the most of their limited time and resources. Nale believes the unit was thorough in re-examining Julie's decades-old case.

"We went over physical evidence, we went over hundreds of pages of reports, we catalogued, and prioritized a bunch of people to contact, and we tracked down as many of those people we could contact to get statements from," Nale said.

Madison police also brought in a detective from the Dane County Sheriff's Office because Julie's body was found outside the city of Madison, but still within the county limits.

Detectives could always benefit from time on most unsolved cases. A little extra work could finally lead to the case being solved. But, 2016 was also a busy year for Madison police trying to solve current cases and the unit had to devote time to the Speerschneider case when it could.

"The Cold Case Unit was in addition to your regular duties so it wasn't like I was handed the Speerschneider case and that was the only thing I worked on," Nale said. "Unfortunately, just the way Madison is structured, a lot of these special units are in addition to your normal duties and at the time I was a detective with the violent crime unit."

To start, all members of the Cold Case Unit would

read the case file. Each investigator would formulate ideas, such as priorities of what to review first and a list of people to contact. Physical evidence was reviewed, reports were read, notes were taken.

"(After that) we're ready to go out and start knocking on doors and talking to people," Nale said. "Those duties got split up among everyone else."

Nale has an idea of what he thinks happened to Julie on that cool, cloudy night in 1979. The case is still considered active, however. He's not sharing that information.

"One thing that I can (share), and I don't think I'm speaking out of class; we were fairly confident that the Speerschneider case was not tied to any of the other cases," Nale said, referring to at least a few of the murders detailed in this book from the late 1970s and early 1980s.

"I know there's been speculation there was a serial killer targeting women around the age of Julie and Christine (Rothschild) near the UW campus," Nale said. "I believe we were fairly confident that was not the case with Julie Speerschneider."

Nale can understand the public speculation. Rothschild and Donna Mraz were both attacked and killed on campus. It's not known for certain if Susan Lemahieu was murdered on UW property, but her body was found in the Arboretum. Could all three murders have been committed by the same killer? Maybe, but considering the Rothschild and Mraz homicides were fourteen years apart, it seems unlikely.

Reopening the Speerschneider case hasn't led to an arrest (as of 2023), but Nale sounded confident detectives are in a better position to solve the case than they were in the early '80s.

"I'm somewhat confident that I think I know what occurred, but I don't want to give too much information on it because I'm hoping at some point, we'll be able to wrap that one up as well," Nale said. "I'm not doing that to be coy, but I would like to see this wrapped up and I would like to have the family be able to say we got some form of justice out of this. But we are fairly confident this was not the work of the same folks who were involved in any of these other cases.

"It's a bit of a standalone event."

One block. What happened to Julie Speerschneider after being dropped off one block from her friend's house?

Could Julie have gotten into the vehicle of someone she knew? Had she met up with a familiar face while hanging out at the 602 Club, they saw her walking alone, and offered to give her a lift?

"That would explain the lack of screaming and people not hearing a disturbance," Nale said.

Was it a friendly, charming stranger? Someone who spotted her at the bar and followed her movements after she left?

"It was these types of cases that forced parents to tell kids, 'Don't talk to strangers, don't get in cars of people who you don't know,'" Nale said. "(Infamous serial killer) Ted Bundy in Florida made his living off of hitchhikers; very common back then."

Frustratingly, many questions remain unanswered. Finally putting the Speerschneider case to bed becomes more challenging as the years fly by. Nale tries to stay optimistic. After all, one phone call, one piece of evidence can finally bring justice to long-suffering families.

"Anything is possible," Nale said. "But the longer we get away from the timeframe when the murder occurred—and it was a challenge back in 2015—it's harder to make that forensic link to someone, with DNA and fingerprints, stuff like that. I don't recall that we had anything to go on in that regard, but I don't recall one hundred percent."

Like many unsolved cases, the veteran detective believes someone knows something.

"You always kind of hope for someone to have a change of heart and they make a phone call," Nale said.

While the 2015-2016 re-examination didn't lead to breaks in the case, it did put Julie's murder under a fresh, new microscope. It could eventually lead to a resolution. The renewed interest also brings hope that the six other cold cases profiled in this book will also receive a new look.

"I wish I could give you a little more on Speerschneider," Nale said as our phone interview concluded.

~

Losing a close friend or family member to murder is an excruciating experience. The mental and physical toll can be relentless. Not many people truly know this feeling. It's a limited club.

Then there are the family and friends of victims whose cases have never been solved. This club is even more exclusive.

Marcia (Speerschneider) Schiffman is in the latter

of the two clubs. Her sister Julie vanished in 1979, only to have her remains found two years later. The killer, whether still at large, dead, or in prison, was never brought to justice. No one has come forward.

More than forty years have passed since Schiffman lost her sister, yet her memory is never far away.

"One of the things you should know is there is hardly a day that goes by that I don't think about Julie," Schiffman said in an email in 2021. "It is mostly good memories."

Schiffman tries to recall the fun times she spent with Julie. It's a stockpile of less than twenty years, but there are plenty of days when the good visions come through. The lighthearted moments. However, there are also times when Julie's murder—the worst memory of those twenty years—returns.

In those moments, the pain comes flooding back.

"Whenever new interest in Wisconsin true crime stories or cold cases are being discussed again, it can cause some unexpected and often unwanted attention," Schiffman said.

In the decades following Julie's murder, local newspapers profiling an unsolved case have often re-printed a list of area cold case homicides. So, there it is again. In bold type: Julie Speerschneider, Madison, 1979. Or, a Madison TV station runs a segment on cold case murders. There's Julie's face, black and white photo, long brown hair, pleasant, unassuming smile, splashed across the screen.

Then come the looks out in public. *Is that? No. ... Yes, I think it is. That's Julie Speerschneider's sister. Remember? The girl that went missing in '79 and was ...*

"Suddenly, you can't go to the grocery store without

the clerk seeing your name and asking about it," Schiffman said.

Those interactions don't happen as much these days. After all, it's been four decades. Marcia has married and changed her last name to Schiffman. But when it does occur, it's jolting.

"Regardless, you open yourself up to being blindsided," Schiffman said.

For Schiffman, she's transported back in time to age sixteen. She's lost her big sister in the worst possible way imaginable. Her teenage world comes crashing down. She doesn't know when it will be whole again. How could that even be possible?

"All of the bad stuff comes flooding back," she said. "It is what happens, at least for me, every time her disappearance and murder is asked about, especially when I'm not expecting it.

"I can only imagine how much more devastating this is for my mother."

Chapter 5

Susan LeMahieu, 1980

The one that fell through the cracks.

That's how retired journalist George Hesselberg describes the unsolved murder case of Susan LeMahieu. Hesselberg covered the case for the *Wisconsin State Journal* in 1980.

LeMahieu was twenty-four when she went missing in December 1979. Her nude body was found a few months later in the UW Arboretum. Unlike most of the other cases profiled in this book, not much is known about LeMahieu's case. Along with Shirley Stewart, who was killed around the same time as Susan, the amount of media coverage pales in comparison to Christine Rothschild's case.

Balousek, the retired Madison reporter, believes different circumstances in those cases impacted some of the coverage.

"Well, I think it's the magnitude of it too," Balousek said. "Christine Rothschild was found right outside of a campus building. That really brought everything home to Madison. And then Donna Mraz ... that was such a tragic case. She was stabbed shortly after midnight. There were actually people who heard her screaming and they tried to come to her rescue. They sort of saw the suspect slip away in the shadows but couldn't pursue him.

"The fact that both happened on campus kind of shocked everybody. Also, the circumstances of the murders. The other women were found later. Some were missing and people didn't even know they were missing until their bodies were found. There was a time-lag there, it wasn't so dramatic."

Unlike the six other women written about here, Susan, known as Susie or Sue to her family and friends, had special needs. Despite her handicap, she lived on her own, renting a room at Allen Hall, 505 N. Frances St., on the UW campus.

On the afternoon of December 15, 1979, Susie left Allen Hall. She was never seen again.

The State Journal did not report her disappearance until January 25, 1980—more than a month after she left Allen Hall. A search through the *Capital Times'* archives show nothing reported about Susie as a missing person. This begs a couple of questions: When did police notify the local press Susie was missing and her family needed help from the public to find her? And, did people care enough to want to find her?

Back in the 1970s and 1980s, there were stigmas about people with special needs. They were often labeled as being "retarded." Thankfully, that nasty word has been mostly stripped from people's vocabulary. But, in 1980, it was very much present. The "r-word" was used to describe Susie in some newspaper accounts of her murder. It was a hurtful and demeaning way to describe someone with a handicap.

Sue LeMahieu

In some ways, people with special needs were looked at as second-class citizens.

There was no question Susie battled challenges, both physically and mentally. She had a slightly disabled left leg, causing her to walk with a limp. Her left arm was also slightly twisted. However, regardless of her obstacles, Susie was bound to live an independent life. She graduated from Madison East High School in 1974. She spent the next several years building a life on her own.

In the late '70s, Allen Hall was a treatment facility for persons with mental and physical handicaps. Allen Hall allowed Susie to live a somewhat normal life; a much better alternative than living in an institution. Sadly, many adults with special needs, if not cared for by a legal guardian, were placed in institutions. They were forgotten about, never taught skills needed to adapt to the outside world and sort of ... lost. Eventually, many died in those institutions without getting a fair shake in the real world.

"Life was not easy for her, but she was a very determined person," said her sister, Lisa, in 2021.

Susie was a motivating force to those who knew her. Lisa, who works as a teacher, tells her students about Susie's determination. She had roadblocks but she didn't let them stand in her way.

However, just as she was building a life of her own, it was tragically cut short.

It's unclear exactly when Susie was killed, but her body was found on April 17, 1980, in the "Lost City" of the Arboretum. The "Lost City" is a marshy area that was once a plot of land earmarked for a Madison subdivision. When plans for the city fell through, the marshy reserve became part of the Arboretum, a vast wooded space on Madison's near west side known for hiking, bird watching and various other recreational activities.

Two joggers found Susie's body, lying in the Arboretum's marshy area under thick brush and about a hundred and fifty feet from a parking lot. She was discovered about a mile from the Arboretum's east entrance. The joggers reported their findings to the Madison Police Department a day later. Police believe they waited to report finding the body because they were too scared of what they had found or weren't sure if it was human remains.

Susie's body was identified using dental records. A ring on one of her fingers also helped confirm it was Susie.

Susie's body was transported to the Wisconsin State Crime Lab for further testing. Since the body was badly decomposed, her cause of death was ruled "inconclusive."

Initially, pathologist Dr. Billy Bauman considered her death accidental. However, upon further investigation, police stopped short of ruling it a homicide, but could admit her death was "suspicious."

Madison Police Captain Richard Cowan told Hesselberg, "We have some ideas as to what the cause of death was, but that won't be made public until further information is developed."

To pursue the probable homicide, police "partially activated" the Dane County Major Crime Unit, which included detectives from UW-Madison, the city of Madison, and the county sheriff's office. So many questions swirled through detectives' minds. Was Susie abducted? Did she go with someone voluntarily? If taken, was she murdered shortly after? Was she killed in the Arboretum or somewhere else and her body transported to the "Lost City?"

For police, even determining how Susie was killed was difficult due to decomposition. And, it's difficult to find news reports with many details of how she died.

The one that fell through the cracks.

Tragedy Hits Family Again

As if Susie's disappearance wasn't enough to shock her family, the discovery of her body and likely murder was another harsh blow.

It wasn't the first time the LeMahieu family dealt with gut-wrenching tragedy. When Susie was ten years old, in 1966, two of her brothers—Douglas and William—died accidentally in the basement of the family's east side residence. They were found in an abandoned refrigerator.

Her parents, Ruth and Gary, lived apart at the time

of Susie's death; Ruth in Madison and Gary in Mauston, a small-town northwest of Madison. Two young sisters, Lori and Lisa, still lived at home in Madison with Ruth, while an older sister, Cindy, was married and lived in Madison. A brother, Robert, resided in Marshfield in central Wisconsin.

On Monday, April 21, in private services at Madison's Schroeder Funeral Home, Susie was laid to rest. Ruth and Gary said goodbye to another child far too soon.

Possible Suspects

Part of being independent was the ability for Susie to get out of her small Allen Hall room, hit some of the bars in Madison, and socialize. She was friendly and enjoyed meeting people. Susie was a fixture in the downtown and east side Madison areas, including King Street, Main Street, State Street, and Williamson Street.

On April 12, 1979, however, she crossed paths with the wrong person.

Susie was allegedly assaulted and "beat up" by Percy Lee Love, a forty-year-old Madison man. The assault was reported to police and Love was charged with battery. A few months after the beating, Susie was ready to testify against Love in court. He was determined for that not to happen.

Love spotted Susie walking through a tavern parking lot on August 24. He confronted her. Love wanted to make it clear to Susie that she was not to testify against him.

"I'll kill you or have someone else do it," Love threatened.

Jolted and frightened, Susie reported the threat to

police. Love was arrested and charged with threatening to injure a witness. In the late '70s, in Wisconsin, that charge carried a five-year prison sentence and a $10,000 fine, equivalent to nearly $40,000 in 2022.

Susie didn't cower away from pressing charges against Love when he attacked her and reported the threat to police. She didn't back down from anyone despite her handicaps.

The incidents with Love carried only a small news brief in the September 6, 1979 edition of the *Capital Times*. But, for Susie's murder case, the implications could be huge. Did investigators look into Love after Susie was murdered? He was never named publicly as a suspect. Did Love make good on his threat to have Susie killed or was it an isolated outburst? Were his words simply bluster?

While it's interesting to ponder if Love had any connection to Susie's murder, police considered two other suspects, at least publicly. Henry Lee Lucas (again) was pinpointed as a possible suspect. His penchant for picking up and murdering hitchhikers and his hundreds of "confessions" fit the LeMahieu case, assuming she was abducted, killed, and left at the Arboretum. The kidnapping and murder also occurred in the same time span as the other homicides Lucas is linked to, such as Julie Hall (1978) and Julie Speerschneider (1979).

Also, around that time, another serial killer was inflicting terror across the Midwest. Edward W. Edwards had killed couple Timothy Hack and Kelly Drew, both nineteen, in 1980 in Jefferson County, directly east of Dane County. The case remained cold for nearly three decades until DNA testing tied Edwards to the double homicide in 2009.

By then, the seventy-six-year-old Edwards was confined to a wheelchair and depended on an oxygen tube to breathe. It was hard to picture this elderly frail man being a deranged monster, but he was. Edwards was linked to several other murders, including three in Ohio.

Edwards received a life sentence for the Wisconsin murders. He was sentenced to death in Ohio for murders there in March 2011. He died in prison of natural causes less than a month later. Edwards was spared from lethal injection by a matter of months.

Edwards' timeline places him in Wisconsin when Susie went missing and was found in the spring of 1980. He fled the state in September 1980 after police questioned him about the Hack/Drew murder. After his arrest in the murder of the young couple, Dane County detectives looked into Edwards as a suspect in the LeMahieu murder.

Steve Gilmore, lieutenant of detectives for the county sheriff's office, admitted nailing Edwards for Susie's homicide was a long shot.

"I don't think it's going to pan out for us," Gilmore told the *Capital Times* in 2009.

In discussing another Dane County cold case—the 1998 unsolved slaying of Catholic priest Alfred Kunz—Gilmore said it's difficult to make an arrest when detectives know a suspect cannot be proven guilty beyond a reasonable doubt.

"That's the threshold. I don't think we'll ever get over the hurdle on that one."

Not only was there not a lot of research to be found on

the LeMahieu case, current departments in Dane County didn't have any new information when contacted in 2021. And, since the Intra-County Task Force was dissolved years after the murder, it's unclear who has all the evidence in Susie's case. Her body was found on UW property, but the UWPD didn't acknowledge her case when asked about it through email. Its possible evidence could be still spread throughout UW, the Dane County Sheriff's Office, and the Madison Police Department.

Or, it could simply be ... lost.

CHAPTER 6

Shirley Stewart, 1980

Of the several mysterious cases profiled here, perhaps the most baffling is the case of Shirley Stewart.

The youngest victim of the lost seven, Shirley was only seventeen years old when she went missing on January 2, 1980. Her body was not discovered until more than a year later, in the summer of 1981, in a wooded area north of Madison.

While Shirley's case is certainly fascinating, very little is known about it. Her disappearance wasn't reported in local newspapers until February 14, 1980—nearly a month and a half after she went missing. More disconcerting, unlike the six other victims, not one photo of Stewart was circulated to Madison area media. A deeper internet search of the homicide case doesn't reveal even a grainy headshot of the teenager.

What is known is that Shirley was from Middleton, living at her parents' residence of 1219 Middleton St. at the time of her disappearance. Her father, Keith, reported her missing to local authorities and a two-paragraph news brief appeared in the Metro digest section of the *State Journal.*

Shirley was fairly tall (five-foot-seven) and thin, weighing about a hundred and twenty-five pounds. No other physical descriptions were made public. It was not clear whether she was still attending high school in the winter of 1980.

One aspect of Shirley's life that is known for sure—she was a single mother.

Her daughter, Christina, was born on December 11, 1978 at the Lutheran Hospital in La Crosse, Wisconsin. She arrived–two weeks late–weighing eight pounds, thirteen ounces. At only sixteen, Shirley was thrust into parenthood.

To support her young child, Shirley worked as a maid at the Dean Clinic in Madison. She left her shift on that cold January night and was never seen again. Keith, along with Shirley's mother, Euene, had a gripping fear their daughter had been abducted. Not only did Shirley leave behind a baby girl, barely old enough to be a toddler, but also sisters Luann and Victoria, along with her brother, Mark.

After a frustrating eighteen months and many sleepless nights, the Stewart family's worst fears were realized—Shirley had been murdered.

Her badly decomposed body was found on July 16, 1981, in the town of Westport, along the northwest shore of Lake Mendota. On a pleasant, eighty-degree summer afternoon, four archeology students were mapping out what would become Gaylord Nelson State Park.

The students were walking in a secluded area, densely

covered in forest, and rarely known for human foot traffic. Traveling south of a farm in the Camp Indianola area, the four students ventured about fifty feet into thick forest and came across a shocking sight–human remains. Through dental records, the body was positively identified as Shirley Stewart the following evening.

Due to severe decomposition, the Dane County Coroner's Office couldn't determine how Shirley died, but police felt certain it was through homicide. She was found without clothing on or jewelry of any kind. Donald Scullion, the county's deputy coroner, believed the murderer tried to conceal the body, making it more difficult to find.

"Indications are the body had to be carried into that area, and brush was piled over it in an apparent attempt to conceal the body," Scullion told the *State Journal*.

What struck local investigators was how similar Shirley's case was to the other abductions and murders of the past few years: Julie Speerschneider, Julie Hall, Debra Bennett, and Sue LeMahieu. All five women were left in remote areas and covered in brush or debris to hide the bodies.

Scullion felt strongly the five unsolved murders could be connected.

"The last two deaths (LeMahieu and Stewart) were very related. It could be the same person doing these. The patterns are: Wooded areas, off the road aways, in a concealed area."

Unlike the other victims, however, Shirley didn't frequent the downtown Madison area. Speerschneider, Hall, Bennett and LeMahieu all enjoyed hanging out around Main, King, and Williamson (also known as "Willy Street") areas. Similar to many young women, they liked to go out and socialize; grab a drink with friends at the downtown bars. Shirley was only seventeen when she was abducted, too young to drink legally. She also lived with her family and had a toddler to care for.

Could Shirley have been stalked? It's possible the killer knew what time she left work. When her shift ended that cold night in early January 1980, the perpetrator might have spotted her and made his move. It's also very likely the teenager was kidnapped and killed at random.

Was the killer someone the Stewart family knew? Keith Stewart was a Middleton city council member for several years in the 1970s. He ran for mayor of the city in 1971 but lost. He was well-known throughout the Madison suburb.

On July 21, the same day the Stewart family buried their daughter, more details emerged about her death. Clyde "Bud" Chamberlain, Dane County coroner, said the body showed "no indication of trauma." Officially, her death was listed as "homicide of undetermined origin."

From the autopsy, authorities could conclude that none of Shirley's bones were penetrated by a bullet or knife wound. But Chamberlain didn't rule out that she might have been stabbed or shot to death. The coroner said there was a possibility she could have been strangled.

Balousek, who covered crime for the *State Journal* during the early 1980s, knew Chamberlain well. Chamberlain also felt the five murders between 1976-1981 were likely committed by the same person, according to Balousek.

"A couple of them had been walking home from their jobs when they were abducted. A lot of those (cases) were so similar," Balousek said. "I think the local authorities were convinced it was a serial killer ... 'Bud' Chamberlain certainly was convinced it was a serial killer."

Since Stewart's body was found outside of Madison, the county sheriff's department led the homicide investigation. Middleton Detective Al Subera also continued to work on the case months after the body was found. When contacted for comments about the Stewart case in 2021, a sheriff's office representative didn't offer any new information about the cold case. Similar to the Hall, Speerschneider, and Bennett cases, Stewart's murder is not listed among the "unresolved cases" section on the Dane County Sheriff's Office website.

~

On September 6, 1981, two months after Shirley's body was discovered, her mother, Euene, received full parental rights over Shirley's daughter, Christina.

Christina's father was unknown, according to a notice of hearing termination of parental rights placed in the August 27, 1981 edition of the *State Journal*. With Shirley gone, Euene raised Christina like another daughter. When Euene died in 2002, Christina was listed as one of her three living daughters in her obituary, despite actually being her granddaughter.

Both Shirley and her mother were laid to rest at the Bernard's Catholic Church cemetery in Middleton. As of 2022, Shirley's father, Keith, was still living in Wisconsin. The ninety-two-year-old was listed as residing in Wautoma. He didn't respond to a request for comment about the case.

With little information about Shirley's case available, any news on a possible suspect was also scant. Due to the similarities to the other cases, Henry Lee Lucas' name came up, briefly, but it doesn't appear that Lucas was a serious suspect.

Chapter 7

Donna Mraz, 1982

Donna Mraz was excited for the upcoming weekend.

Mraz, a twenty-three-year-old junior at the University of Wisconsin-Madison, was looking forward to some fun during Fourth of July weekend, 1982. The friendly, outgoing college student pinned a note to a bulletin board at work, inviting co-workers to a party on Friday night. Donna was close with her fellow staff at Bittersweet Restaurant along State Street in downtown Madison. She wanted to let her hair down and have a good time with friends outside of work's nightly grind.

Donna never made it to Friday night.

In a brutal, brazen attack that still resonates with perplexing questions four decades later, Donna Mraz was stabbed multiple times while walking home from work. She was attacked just before midnight on July 1, 1982. Donna was rushed to the nearby University Hospital and Clinics but it was too late. She died about two hours later.

Forty years have passed since the last murder on the

UW campus, yet so many unanswered questions remain. The most glaring—why Donna?

Was she being stalked? Did the killer know her? Was it a random attack? Was he trying to rob her? Was it an attempted sexual assault?

What is known is that Donna was attacked right outside of Camp Randall Stadium. The venerable sports venue, home to the Wisconsin Badgers football team, has been a centerpiece of UW for more than a century. In the middle of summer, however, the stadium was dead quiet. Football season was still two months away. Many students were either home for the summer or staying in off-campus houses or apartments. Most, like Donna, were working summer jobs to help support their college education.

On this warm July night, the large venue cast deep, dark shadows along the adjacent streets and walking paths that hug the stadium. It wouldn't have been difficult for a perpetrator to hide amongst the shadows, hidden by a cloak of darkness, ready to pounce on an unsuspecting victim.

Donna Mraz

Donna was in the wrong place at the wrong time.

Even more heart-wrenching, Donna was about two blocks from home, a house at 1717 Van Hise Ave., when she was attacked. Donna had left work around 11:30 p.m. and taken a bus to a stop near the stadium. She was found forty yards east of Breese Terrace, between the stadium and a practice field.

Donna had suffered a deep stab wound to the left side of her chest: A direct blow to the heart killed her. Donald Scullion, the deputy coroner for the county sheriff's office, said Donna also had stab wounds on her face, chest, and left arm. No doubt she put up a fight. Her life was on the line.

Police reported that Donna was not sexually assaulted, and no belongings were taken from her. She was found holding onto her purse, suggesting she feared being robbed. The Mraz murder was the tipping point of a violent night across Madison. A woman was raped and beaten in a parking lot near the Shuffle Inn off the West Beltline Highway. In the town of Madison, a woman was sexually assaulted in her apartment. Several other incidents were also reported. No arrests were immediately made.

Donna's murder followed three previous stabbings of young women around Madison. Local police, however, were quick to dismiss those incidents as having any relation to the Mraz attack. Jeffrey Frye, a lieutenant with Madison police, told the press there were a "number of dissimilarities" among the cases to be linked. Still, it was enough to put the city on edge.

Much like it was in the spring of 1968.

Donna's murder was the last homicide on the UW

campus since Christine Rothschild was brutally killed in May of '68. The murders occurred fourteen years apart, but Christine and Donna will forever be linked. Both attractive, bright college students full of life. Ambitious. Driven. Academically successful. Well-liked. Admired. Both lives cut down way too soon. And for what? Why?

Why?

The question has burned in the minds of family, friends, and the detectives who worked on these cases for decades. Both cases remain unsolved. Could both homicides be linked to the same attacker? It seems unlikely. While both victims were stabbed, more than fourteen years had passed between the two murders. Would the same person return to UW and do it again? It's not out of the question, but highly unlikely.

Both Christine and Donna were independent young women. And, for the most part, fearless. Christine didn't think twice about taking long walks along campus early in the morning. Donna didn't flinch at the thought of walking home by herself after work. They weren't afraid. Perhaps a little too trusting of the unknown.

"I'm not worried about anything," Donna once told her manager at the Bittersweet.

Life Going Great for Donna

To friends and co-workers, Donna was a bright and bubbly, highly intelligent person. She resonated with a friendly, warm nature. She invited people into her circle and could easily make friends.

Donna had worked at Bittersweet for nearly three

years. She enjoyed spending time with her co-workers. News of her murder hit them hard. On July 2, the day after Donna was attacked, most of her co-workers were sent home. Emotionally rattled, they couldn't possibly focus on serving food and busing tables.

"It's been pretty rough around here," Gene Konitzer, Bittersweet's owner, told the *Capital Times*. "We were all pretty close."

Konitzer said Donna was a model employee with a "dynamite personality, real open and bubbling."

Donna's sudden, shocking death tore a hole through the heart of the mostly young restaurant staff.

"She had a lot of friends," Konitzer said.

"There are some people here whom I wouldn't ask about Donna," said Connie Wyss, a Bittersweet staff member. "They are apt to get pretty emotional."

While she still had several weeks to enjoy summer break, Donna was looking forward to the return of classes in the fall. A business major, she had recently told co-workers that she "finally knew what she wanted to do with her life." In the classroom, Donna knocked out excellent grades. She was on the dean's list.

All aspects of Donna's young life were pointing upward.

"She was doing fine in school, was thinking about changing her major," Konitzer said.

For students going from high school to college, the transition can be bumpy. Not for Donna. A 1977 graduate from Delavan-Darien High School, Donna finished third in her class. She was a member of the National Honor Society and earned the community's $4,000 George W.

Boarg academic scholarship, equivalent to almost $20,000 in 2022. Donna was also an athlete, playing varsity softball and basketball.

Outside of academics and sports, Donna loved music. She was a talented piano player. Known to work hard, she put effort into everything she did.

Donna had the sense to go above and beyond in most aspects of her life. That likely came from her upbringing. When her father, Robert, wasn't busy with work at Sta-Rite Industries in Delavan, he served as the volunteer chief of the Delavan Township Rescue Squad. Along with his wife, Lois, Robert raised Donna and her younger brother, Michael, known as "Mickey," in the small southeast Wisconsin town.

Donna's rural Midwestern childhood likely fostered her humble, kind, hard-working personality.

For Wyss, Donna's murder was extremely surprising. She was someone who "wouldn't hurt anyone."

"Everyone was her sweetie. She was good friends with everyone here," Wyss told the *Wisconsin State Journal*. "I really thought a lot of her.

"It has been pretty gloomy around here."

Donna shared the house on Van Hise Avenue with two female roommates. Severely shaken by the tragedy, both declined to talk to reporters. Elsie Johnson, who lived next door to Donna and her roommates, said the students were quiet, respectful neighbors. Nice girls who didn't throw loud parties or were involved in any kind of trouble.

Romantically, it didn't appear Donna had a boyfriend. It's unclear if she was dating anyone at the time of her death. She was outgoing and sociable but seemed laser-focused on school and work in the summer of '82.

Much like Christine Rothchild more than a decade earlier.

Details Try to Piece Together What Happened

So close, yet so far.

Similar to the dark shadows he emerged from, whoever attacked Donna escaped back into the darkness of night. He still hasn't been found.

Those who came to Donna's rescue, though, said they saw a man running from the scene. They were able to piece together a vague description, but details were scant.

Around midnight, several young men living in apartments near Camp Randall heard the piercing screams of a woman in trouble. The woman screamed several more times. Neighbors in the area knew something was wrong. These weren't the screams of a drunk student blowing off steam. They were of someone being attacked.

"There's definitely a difference in the two, and you can tell when you hear it," said Madison police officer Mike Hanson in 2021.

Startled by the screaming, a twenty-two-year-old male student went to an apartment window to see what was happening: a woman running, then collapsing to the ground. He ran from his apartment down to Donna, bleeding, gasping for breath along the walkway. She was in bad shape. The young man called the paramedics. An ambulance was on the scene within minutes.

Another witness, working on the third floor of the Electrical and Computer building, told police he heard several screams, prompting him to look out a window. Three minutes passed when he spotted a person running from Camp Randall's driveway to the UW Fieldhouse. However, he couldn't provide police with an accurate description.

After Donna's murder the Major Case Unit—the same city, county and university police force that banded together to investigate the Rothschild case—dove into action. About eighteen officers were assigned full-time to the case with another six or eight lending assistance. Working out of the university's Department of Protection and Security at 101 N. Mills Street, they poured all their energy into solving this shocking homicide. The unit started receiving calls and pieced together various tips from the public, but any solid leads were hard to come by.

"We are trying to run down various pieces of information," Lieutenant Jeffrey Frye from the Madison Police Department told the press.

Frye said within twenty-four hours after the murder, quite a few calls came in, moving the investigation "a little further" along.

Marv Balousek, covering the crime beat for the *State Journal*, just missed being called to the scene. He had left work to go home around midnight on July 2. The next day, however, Balousek was deep in reporter mode, gathering all the information he could and scouring the neighborhood near Donna's house.

"The next day I was out walking Randall Street, knocking on doors, seeing if people knew anything," he said. "For Mraz, I didn't have much contact with the family. I wanted to find people who had been there on the scene. I wanted to find neighbors who had seen or heard anything."

On July 3, in one of Balousek's follow-up stories, he reported police had asked the twenty-two-year-old student who ran to help Donna if he would be placed under hypnosis. The Major Crime Unit hoped the Milwaukee man could have his memory jogged, providing a vital clue in the case. While he saw Donna scream and crumble to the pavement, he said he did not see her attacker.

The student told police he "went out right away." When he met up with Donna, it was a sight no one would ever forget. Blood poured down from Donna's chest and arms. She suffered a deep wound to her left arm and there was dampness on her chest. Blood began pooling from another stab wound.

Being the age before cell phones, the student had to run back up to his apartment to call an ambulance. He returned with another man. They wrapped Donna in a blanket. Gasping for air, the student tried to resuscitate her. After about three minutes, the paramedics arrived. They stayed on the scene for another twenty minutes, stabilizing Donna before transporting her to University Hospital.

With UW Police Chief Ralph Hanson vacationing with his family in Maine, Lieutenant Gary Moore initially led the investigation. Balousek liked Moore. He was often a treasure trove of information. A crime reporter's dream. Sometimes, however, he provided too much information.

"There were times when I covered court (news) where

he would say something that I wouldn't print, so I kind of protected him a little bit. He was just so open about everything, and I wanted to protect him," Balousek said.

Balousek's news stories carried vivid details of how Donna was attacked and what transpired after the fatal encounter.

"Some of the other detectives were bristling because he held a press conference and just laid it all out," he said of Moore.

The assailant did not steal money or try to remove Donna's clothing, but that didn't necessarily rule out a robbery or attempt at sexual assault.

"It could have been a sexual assault, it could have been a plain assault, it could have been a robbery attempt," Moore said in his press conference.

Still, Moore was frustrated that additional leads—really, any solid leads—hadn't come through. Especially since bystanders rushed to help Donna so quickly. The attacker simply struck with sudden urgency and fled into the night. Curtailing investigators' efforts even more, the attacker made sure to keep the murder weapon, a knife, with him when he sprinted from the scene.

The young man who ran to help Donna said she didn't say anything. Likely in shock, she found it difficult to speak.

Police hoped that more witnesses would come forward as well. Yes, it was close to midnight during summer break, and fewer students were on campus, but someone had to have seen something. Based on reports, Donna screamed several times. The screaming concerned some neighbors while others believed it was no big deal.

"We had somebody that saw a shadow around the stadium but absolutely no description," Moore said.

Somewhat surprisingly, Moore told reporters Donna did not take the route around Camp Randall regularly. Sometimes, after work, she would take a bus closer to her house, grab a ride with a friend, or walk the entire way. This information makes it harder to believe Donna was stalked by her murderer for days or weeks. Was the attack simply a random, vicious act?

While hypnosis is a controversial, rarely used method in policing, detectives believed it could help the case's key witness recall something vital to crack open a lead. Balousek wrote, however, the method can sometimes do more harm than good.

"Critics contend hypnosis can irrevocably taint the memory of a witness who may be unable to distinguish later between actual memory and the recollections created during hypnosis."

Another aspect that threw a wrench in the early stages of the investigation–the Fourth of July weekend. Police tried to track down witnesses and bystanders but many had left Madison for the weekend. They reviewed a video of Donna being hauled into the ambulance, hoping to identify people huddled around the scene.

Investigators were also planning to interview the twenty-two-year-old student that ran to Donna's aid a second time. He also left for the holiday weekend. He hadn't decided if he wanted to be put under hypnosis to recall details of that terrible night.

The bloody attack and murder left him emotionally drained. He saw a young woman struggling for her life and could do little to help. "Spooked" by the incident, according to one of his roommates, the student immediately locked all the doors to the apartment early Friday morning.

Most of the neighborhood around Breese Terrace felt the same. Many residents didn't want to discuss the murder. Some couldn't sleep after the attack. A student told Balousek he stayed up all night, parked beside a window, watching cars drive by.

Eerily similar to fourteen years earlier when Christine Rothschild was stabbed to death outside Sterling Hall, the shockwaves of murder at a typically calm, safe university rippled throughout campus. The shock reverberated through Madison. It remained a city on edge for a while after Donna was slain.

Meanwhile, detectives continued to probe for breaks in the case. Moore told the press the crime unit was taking "a long look" at an incident from a few nights prior to the Mraz murder. A woman was assaulted near Murray and Regent Street. A few details in that attack mirrored the Mraz case.

On the Sunday before Donna was killed, a woman was grabbed from behind by a knife-wielding attacker. She was able to fight him off but was cut on the right leg. Terrified, she broke free and ran to a nearby home. But investigators didn't have a solid description of the attacker.

Detectives were also combing through files, pinpointing possible suspects with violent backgrounds. They were hoping a few matched the profile of Donna's murderer.

Murder, Assaults Frighten City

As if the Donna Mraz murder wasn't enough for the city to digest, a series of violent attacks on women put Madison on notice.

In less than a month before Donna was viciously attacked, at least ten women reported sexual assaults. In two of the cases, perpetrators used knives. Detectives thought a few of the attacks were related and were trying to connect the assaults to Donna's murder.

In at least three of the attacks, the assailant was described as a Black man, about five-foot-nine and weighing around a hundred and seventy pounds with a short Afro, no facial hair, and sporting a medium complexion. Victims described him as having a high-pitched voice and possibly left-handed.

It's likely Donna didn't know her attacker, similar to the other assaulted women. Police were trying to determine if the incidents were all just random acts of violence from a crazed perpetrator. Regardless, young women around Madison did not feel safe, especially UW-Madison students.

"There is a sense of vulnerability among co-eds at the University of Wisconsin," Assistant Dean of Students Mary Rouse told the *State Journal*. "I feel a sense of tragedy and a sense of rage that in 1982 the streets do not belong equally to men and women."

Meanwhile, in Delavan, a private funeral service was held. Donna was laid to rest on July 6 at Roselawn Memory Gardens in Walworth County.

An inscription on her headstone reads:

DEARLY LOVED IN LIFE
DEARLY LOVED STILL

There's no question that the small community where Donna grew up was shaken by the sudden, tragic loss. A Mraz family neighbor told the *Capital Times* he knew Donna since birth.

"The whole community is upset. We want to see the person responsible caught."

In 1980, the university surveyed five hundred and one students and asked if they felt safe on campus. Almost a quarter said they did not feel safe. Nearly thirty percent reported they didn't feel safe at night. Points around campus that caused concern were State Street, Capitol Square, Langdon, Johnson, and Mifflin streets and the area around Camp Randall Stadium where Donna was killed.

The survey didn't specify respondents by gender, but it's believed women expressed the most fear. Rouse and other university officials advocated for students, especially females, to walk home with a friend, particularly at night.

"We have the perennial problem of students believing this can't happen to them," Rouse said.

In a comment that could be construed as victim blaming, Rouse said, "Donna Mraz was walking alone at midnight. Thousands of times, we have discouraged women from walking alone at night in poorly lit areas."

In 1982, Rouse was also leading a committee pushing for night classes to start and conclude simultaneously, developing an emergency telephone network and increasing lighting across campus.

Public sentiment also called for improving safety on the large Midwestern campus. On July 12, the *Capital Times* published a letter from Diane Worzala, a mother and local resident, pleading for UW-Madison to find ways to make the university safer.

> *I am tired of being afraid – afraid for my daughters, afraid for their friends, and even afraid for myself. The tragic death of Donna Mraz is just one more horrifying example of why so many Madison women live in fear. Surely it is not beyond the intelligence or determination of this community to devise ways to guarantee the safety of its women.*
>
> *As a start, I urge that your readers contribute to the Women's Transit Authority so that this essential service can survive and expand; that every neighborhood association call a special meeting to discuss steps toward making its territory more secure, including the possible establishment of volunteer patrols; and that every business that is open at night explore ways to ensure that its employees get home safely after work.*

Detectives, meanwhile, forged ahead in their investigation. Following the Fourth of July weekend, police were hoping to track down people close to Donna who talked to her in the weeks leading up to her murder. They also wanted to speak to women who may have been confronted by a man near Camp Randall in recent days.

Investigators did not have a strong description of the murderer, but on July 7 they released a sketch of a person of interest. The man, a white male, about twenty-five-to-thirty years old, was seen near the crime scene just before the murder. He was about five-foot-nine with straight dark brown hair and a full beard and mustache. He was seen wearing a white T-shirt with green stripes, along with dark pants. The man was spotted walking along a sidewalk next to the stadium.

Gary Moore, from the UW police, made it clear the man was not a suspect, but at least it provided detectives a small bit of direction. The drawing yielded numerous calls to the Major Crime Unit but failed to deliver any concrete evidence. Police also wanted to talk to the man to gauge whether he saw anything suspicious before Donna was attacked.

Moore said four or five young men, after hearing Donna's terrifying screams and seeing her fall, rushed out to do everything they could to help her. However, by the time they arrived, her assailant was nothing more than a shadow buried in the darkness of night.

"They were so close, yet so far," Moore said of them getting a clear look at the murderer.

By July 9, about twenty investigators from the Major Crime Unit were on the case. They developed a psychological profile of the killer in an attempt to track down possible suspects. The unit was also trying to hunt down any bloody clothing or materials from the scene, along with the murder weapon. Police believed Donna was attacked with a large knife. It was nowhere to be found.

Similar to the Rothschild homicide, all vacations for detectives were put on hold to pour more investigative resources into finding Donna's killer. Captain John Heibel, manager of Madison Police Department's Investigative Services Bureau, told reporters the Mraz case was the unit's "top priority."

"It gets our first attention," he said.

The unit was believed to have been formed in the wake of Christine's murder. The three-agency bureau was only activated in cases with intense public interest. The group of investigators also worked on the Debra Bennett and Julie Hall cases.

Bloody Jeans, Possible Clue?

A week after Donna was murdered, police discovered a clue, hoping it would lead to a break in the case: Bloody jeans.

The pair of jeans were found about three blocks from where the UW student was attacked. The blood-stained blue jeans, found by a UW student and his wife, were lying across a tree near the railroad tracks in the 1800 block of Keyes Avenue. They were found in a bushy location and appeared to be new. Local police reported the jeans were damp, likely from recent rainfall, and had blood stains on the front and backs of both pant legs, according to the *Capital Times*. The pants measured thirty-four inches around the waist and thirty-one inches down the leg.

The Major Crime Unit decided to ship the jeans to the State Crime Laboratory in Madison for analysis. Was that human blood smeared across the pants? The bloody jeans weren't much but with a week gone by since the homicide and few viable leads trickling in, it was something.

Sharon D. Pitman, a staff writer for the *Capital Times*, summed up what most people were thinking about the possible clue. "The jeans could turn out to be just another in a series of frustrating dead ends police have explored. On the other hand, they could be the first substantial breakthrough in the investigation."

Police also intensely examined the area where the jeans were found, hoping to find the murder weapon. They had no luck.

Lieutenant George Miller, from the Dane County Sheriff's Office, said while investigators still had not cracked open the case, they were receiving "many, many tips" through phone calls. "They are checking them out no matter how minute or remote they may seem," wrote *Capital Times* reporter Mike Miller.

Through the investigation, it was also discovered Donna cut through the area near Camp Randall at least a few times on her way to her house. Did the killer know she sometimes took an alternate route?

To add more suspense, the crime lab couldn't start analyzing the jeans for a few days. The lab's micro-serology department was in charge of the examination but was also working on evidence from other homicide cases ready to go to court. Due to state budget cuts, the lab was short-staffed. The same bulk of work had to be completed by fewer employees.

Finally, more than a week after the jeans were found, the results came through ... rabbit blood.

Rabbit blood.

The blood was not Donna's or anyone else's. It wasn't even human.

Despite the disappointment, Miller brushed it off. He told reporters the crime unit "never really connected (the jeans) to the case, although it was a possibility." He claimed the case was not at a standstill, but with zero solid leads at hand, where did it go from here?

On July 16, two weeks after Donna was murdered, leaders from the crime unit met to reassess the case and determine the next steps. Precious time was ticking away. The unsolved murder of Donna Mraz was slipping through their hands.

City Pushes Safety Measures

With the spike in violent attacks aimed at women–peaked by the brazen murder of Mraz–the city of Madison and the university scrambled to find ways to make the city safer.

City officials, led by a sexual assault committee, considered expanding Madison's bus service to include late-night hours, but that was deemed too expensive. Expanding the service to 12:10 a.m. would have cost city taxpayers almost $91,000. Pushing out the buses to another later shift, say 1:20 a.m., would have carried a $210,337 price tag. The night she was attacked, Donna apparently missed the last bus from the Capitol Square traveling west. It ended around 11:15 p.m. That bus ride might have saved her life.

Nonetheless, the bus service extension plan was still on the table. If approved, it was slated to begin on January 1, 1983.

Local cab companies suggested Madison and Dane County provide vouchers for women working late to receive taxi service. City budget proposals called for less street lighting in Madison, an idea fiercely rejected by the sexual assault committee.

Complete Channel TV, broadcasting throughout Madison, donated $200 of free television time to publicize the need for more late-night public transportation. Richard Wegner, Complete Channel's executive vice president, was fed up with all the recent attacks on women. Something had to be done to stop it.

"I'm a lifelong resident of Madison and I've watched this problem of sexual assaults get worse and worse," Wegner told the *Capital Times*. "It's running at epidemic proportions, and it's an outrage."

Another problem was that many young women around Madison weren't aware of transportation programs already available. The publicity effort hoped to educate them about resources. The Committee on Sexual Assault planned to have flyers and posters up around UW-Madison and other parts of the city before registration week at the university.

In addition, more funding was considered for the Women's Transit Authority, a program advocating for late-night workers to share rides or companies to cover the cost of cab fare and subsidies for late-night transportation. The *State Journal* reported that the WTA provided free rides to more than 22,000 women within a few miles of the Capitol in 1981.

Publicly, calls for increasing transportation service were rising. In late August, the *State Journal* penned an editorial pushing for more late-night options. The editorial did concede, however, that "mass" transportation should be for all, not just the benefit of the few, hence the high cost to extend the service. The piece also pointed out that buses don't drop women off directly in front of their homes. They still must walk a short distance to get inside and even then, safety is not guaranteed.

"By encouraging women to remain out later, extended bus service could increase the number of women making short but potentially dangerous walks downtown and, in their neighborhoods," the editorial argued.

While the recent rise in random street attacks was cause for concern, the paper said there wasn't a quick fix to the problem. The editorial also claimed women should take more precautions to ensure their own safety.

"The city should support all reasonable and affordable efforts to prevent assaults," the editorial stated. "The bus extension is neither, but city officials should remain open to exploring alternatives."

In September, Madison Mayor Joel Skornicka unveiled a plan for women to buy forty dollars' worth of coupons for cab fares from the city clerk for twenty dollars. Women could cash in the coupons exclusively from 10:00 p.m. to 2:30 a.m. At the end of each month, Madison would pay back cab companies for whatever money remained on the fares.

The *Capital Times* praised the mayor's plan in an editorial: "Let's try Skornica's experiment for a year. If it helps combat a crime that has turned the lives of many women into nightmares and caused others to walk in fear, the investment will have paid for itself many times over."

Reward Hopes to Help Case

In late July, in an effort to move the case forward, an

anonymous donor offered a $5,000 reward to anyone who provided information about the murder. The donation was sent to the University of Wisconsin Foundation and was set to expire on July 30, 1983.

If anyone involved in the investigation was becoming deterred, they weren't showing it. Not publicly at least.

"I'm not discouraged at this point," Lieutenant Gary Moore told the press. "I'm still in a very positive frame of mind. We've had suspects and still continue to have them. We've had a couple of people look very good to us in the past week."

But as the days and weeks passed, concern crept in that, similar to the Rothschild case fourteen years earlier, Donna Mraz's killer would not face justice.

"When I left the murder scene, that thought crossed my mind," Moore said.

By the summer of 1982, police had looked into more than three thousand leads connected to the Rothschild case. Nothing substantial was found: The murderer was still on the run, and the murder weapon was nowhere to be found. Eventually, as an unsolved case grows colder, less time is devoted to the case. Detectives move on to other crimes. By the early '80s, local detectives were only spending a few days a year digging into the Rothschild murder. In Donna's case, less than a month after her murder, investigators were already dropping off, from twenty at the start of the case to about ten at the end of July.

Despite the roadblocks, the Major Crime Unit insisted it was not at a dead end. George Miller, from the Dane County Sheriff's Office, said several suspects were eliminated from the investigation.

Miller told the *Capital Times*, "We still have a couple of possible suspects, but whether that will turn up anything I don't know."

In the weeks following the murder, local law enforcement also looked for ways to reduce crime. Not only was Dane County reeling from the Mraz murder, but earlier in 1982, Donna McCormick, a ten-year-old girl, was brutally killed. McCormick's case would eventually be solved.

Dane County Sheriff Jerome Lacke proposed starting a citizen crime patrol to spot suspicious activity. Lacke said the patrol would consist of various groups of local volunteers tasked with calling the sheriff's department if they thought a crime was occurring. Members of the task force would drive around the area between 8:00 p.m. and midnight on Friday and Saturday nights. The volunteers' vehicles would be affixed with a magnetic sign, provided by the sheriff's department, reading "Sheriff's Security Patrol."

While the patrol would have no power to arrest criminals, Lacke believed the citizens could help in stopping crimes before they happened. Donna was attacked just before midnight. A citizens' patrol might not have saved her life, but someone could have spotted the killer before he ran off.

Police Put Onus on Women to Stay Safe

Still, with all the ideas of more late-night transportation, citizen patrols and other means to keep the public safe, police felt women needed to do more to stand up to attackers.

They needed to get streetwise.

That was the sentiment from Karen Hanson, a UW police detective, who told the *Capital Times* she had stressed for ten years that women must take precautions. Hanson claimed it all fell on deaf ears. Most students tuned it out.

Referring to the Mraz homicide, Hanson said, "If anything good can come out of a tragedy like that, perhaps it's that there will be an increased awareness on campus."

Hanson was one of about ten officers still pursuing the case in the Major Crime Unit by late August. The thirty-six-year-old detective believed UW-Madison, with a high concentration of young women students, was like a shiny red target for sex offenders. Hanson said many of the students are kind and helpful. Trusting, to a fault.

"The creeps on the street know that," she said.

The detective said two hundred and twenty-seven sexual assaults were reported in Dane County in 1981. Hanson felt the actual number was much higher. While she didn't want women on campus feeling fearful, she wanted them to be aware of their surroundings.

The early '80s was a more innocent time than today, but Hanson felt that many young women believed a sexual assault could not happen to them. What's still true today, as Hanson pointed out in the interview, most women students at UW-Madison either come from large cities and feel Madison is a nice, safe, little town or hail from small, rural communities in the Midwest and don't find it necessary to take precautions.

Donna fell into the latter category, a small-town girl from Delavan who feared almost no one.

"It's really tragic," Hanson said. "The kids from small towns are just sitting ducks because they're so trusting and so naïve."

Every year, the UW police offered security training sessions at dorms across campus. Attendance was bleak. "Frustrating," Hanson said.

The article also listed several tips women could use to prevent an attack, including not walking alone at night and traveling in well-lit areas. Ironically, one of the tips was similar to what a UW officer told Christine Rothschild more than fourteen years earlier when she reported someone stalking her ... buy a whistle.

July 1982 saw twenty-two reported sexual assaults in Madison, but the number of assaults dropped to seventeen in August, likely due to the intense investigation surrounding the Mraz case.

"Intensive questioning of possible suspects in the case may have intimidated potential assailants from committing sexual assaults during August," reported the *State Journal*.

By late summer, investigators surmised that the spike in sexual assaults in June and July weren't connected to the Mraz murder, due to the "nature of the attack." Captain Richard Josephson, who was interviewed in 2021 about the Rothschild case, was serving as head of investigative services for Dane County at the time Donna was murdered. As the initial investigation drew colder, Josephson told the *State Journal* it could take a "stroke of luck or an unlikely piece of evidence that falls into place" to help break open the frustrating case.

Stalker Haunts Camp Randall Area

Camp Randall Stadium packs in more than eighty thousand crazed football fans every Saturday when the beloved Wisconsin Badgers hit the field. The sprawling stadium commands a large presence in the center of the UW campus, blanketing the area around it with vast, dark shadows.

It was the ideal place for Lonnie Taylor to stalk unsuspecting women.

In the early-morning hours of October 25, 1982, Taylor, just eighteen years old, allegedly stalked a woman outside the stadium. When a bystander tried to stop him, Taylor pulled a knife on him, according to a police report. The witness saw Taylor following the woman on a ten-speed bicycle along the 1300 block of Regent Street. When she turned onto Randall Street, Taylor sped up to catch up to her.

The witness walked up to Taylor and the two men exchanged comments. Taylor turned to face him, holding a "banana" stiletto knife armed with a five-inch blade. Taylor allegedly stepped toward the witness, barking, "You better leave or I'll slash your face up."

The man, unarmed and not wanting to take any chances, sprinted away from the encounter. He dashed into a nearby convenience store and called police. Officers caught up with Taylor shortly afterward. He told police his name was "Robert Williams" and he lived at "1849 Fisher St." Both were made up. Taylor's actual address was 1850 Fisher St. in Madison.

Before he was stopped by the witness, Taylor tried entering a home where four young women resided. He snuck between two houses on Randall Avenue and tried prying open a window.

Taylor probably shouldn't have been out roaming the streets in the first place. The teenager was free from jail, having posted bond and a seven-thousand-dollar cash bail for a December 1981 incident in which he allegedly raped and robbed a woman at a store on Madison's south side. Taylor, along with two other men, broke into and burglarized the store. Taylor and another assailant, according to police, raped the woman at gunpoint, threatening to kill her.

The late October stalking incident occurred within two blocks of Donna's murder. Police didn't want to jump to conclusions, but they did question Taylor about the Mraz case. Detectives were also hoping to talk to the woman Taylor was stalking.

The knife Taylor used to threaten the witness had a thin blade. Police were confident the knife involved in Donna's death also had a thin blade. As he awaited charges in the October 25 incident, Taylor was being held without bail due to the other charges from the alleged armed robbery and rape.

As the calendar flipped to 1983, other alleged rapists were considered suspects, but eventually ruled out. In January, twenty-three-year-old James C. Morgan was charged with three counts of first-degree sexual assault. Morgan reportedly held a woman at knife point while he raped her.

The victim told police Morgan tracked her down in a parking lot off Badger Parkway, forced her inside her home, and threatened her with a thirteen-inch butcher knife, all while sexually assaulting her.

A key comment Morgan made to the woman during the attack sparked police interest.

"He told her that if she didn't do what he said that

he would cut her up like he had done the other girls," the criminal complaint stated.

Less than a week before, another twenty-three-year-old woman was assaulted and slashed with a knife at Hughes Place, just a few blocks from Badger Parkway. The UW police, however, didn't see the increase in sexual attacks with large knives as a direct line to the Mraz case.

"It's speculation," Captain Robert Hartwig told the *State Journal.*

In March, local papers published 1982 crime statistics from UW-Madison. The Mraz murder marred an otherwise typical year for campus police and security. And, as the months drifted by, the unsolved case hung over the minds of detectives.

"It was a tragedy," Ralph Hanson, UW chief of police, told reporters.

For Hanson, the pain of another unsolved slaying of a young female student was difficult to grasp. But, unlike the Rothschild case in 1968, Hanson was not one of the first officers on the scene. He was on vacation with his family, about 1,500 miles away in the Northeast.

Hanson, despite being on vacation, always made a point of checking in with his staff. Long before the luxury of cell phones, texts, and email, there were payphones. Mike Hanson, Ralph's son, recalled his dad popping into phone booths at various gas stations and rest stops along the trip.

"These days my dad would be so confused with texting and emails, he just wasn't a technology guy," Hanson said in 2021. "He would stop at payphones, put quarters in to call back to headquarters to get any updates in general. It wasn't every day, but every few days."

In early July 1982, as the family was heading home, Chief Hanson hadn't called headquarters in two or three days. Hanson figured he would catch up with officers after he got back. When he picked up the local papers left on the family's porch during their trip, he turned to the front page and scanned the headlines. Shock swept over his face.

"UW CO-ED MURDERED"

Hanson wasted no time. He jumped into his car and rushed to the UW police station. Thoughts of 1968 and the horror of a slain Christine Rothschild swirled through his mind.

How could this happen again?

"We unloaded the car, and we didn't see dad for a few days because he was so entrenched in this," Mike Hanson said. "Again, another case of a young female murdered, and he felt responsible to ensure, because this happened on campus, that this gets solved."

Hanson died in 1996, waiting for both Rothchild's and Mraz's killers to face justice.

"There was newer technology than in the Rothschild case but still not enough to grab the suspect," Mike Hanson said of the Mraz murder. "That remains an open investigation with UWPD. The Mraz family has members still alive. It would be important, like Rothschild, to bring this case to closure."

Donna's Body Exhumed for Evidence

Indeed, Taylor matched the criminal profile of Donna's killer, but with no solid evidence linking him to the murder, police officially ruled him out as a suspect in early November.

"(Lonnie) Taylor has been interviewed and at this time nothing has been developed that strongly links him with the murder investigation," Hartwig said.

Yet, investigators had somebody they were tracking. They weren't about to tell the public who it was. Police took a bold step in the fall of 1983 by exhuming Donna's body for clues. They wanted to compare bite marks from a possible suspect to Donna's teeth. It was believed Donna, who had some knowledge of martial arts, fought her killer and bit him before suffering a wound to the chest. Donna had confided in friends that she wanted to learn self-defense tactics after she was scared by a small burglary. Investigators hired a private lab to create a three-dimensional reconstruction of the bite marks.

Unfortunately for detectives, the results were inconclusive.

"I don't know if they matched or not but it wasn't enough to bring him to trial," Balousek said. "They just didn't have enough evidence."

Detectives had a person of interest in mind, although no one was being held in custody. In the weeks following the murder, police canvassed the area near Camp Randall several times to locate anyone who saw or heard anything suspicious the night Donna was attacked. They also brought in many people with violent backgrounds to grill them on the murder. No solid leads transpired.

By November 1983, only one UW detective remained on the Mraz case.

"As it stands at this time, that's all that's necessary," Hartwig said.

While most investigators from the Major Crime Unit had dropped off the case, it didn't mean Donna's murder was losing interest. On November 5, the *State Journal* reported an anonymous donor had doubled reward money for information to ten thousand dollars. Hartwig hoped more money would lead to a break in the case, someone coming forward. It did not.

One positive that did come through from the tragedy was the expansion of safe transportation for women. After months of haggling and cutting through red tape, women in Madison seeking reliable rides late at night could feel safer by the end of 1983.

Case Haunts Police

Friday, December 14, 1984 was a bittersweet day for Detective Marion "Dusty" Rhodes of the Dane County Sheriff's Office.

Retirement after a long, fulfilling career is always met with a twinge of joy and sadness. Rhodes had mixed emotions. After twenty-one years as a detective, Rhodes closed many cases. He was especially proud of convicting Roger Lange of the 1982 murder and sexual assault of ten-year-old Paula McCormick and putting him behind bars for a very long time.

There was one case that gnawed at him, though. Rhodes wasn't able to solve Donna Mraz's murder.

The veteran detective was angry. In his gut, he knew who killed Donna. But what could he do? There simply was not enough evidence to make an arrest.

"There's a lot of anguish inside," Rhodes told Sharon D. Pitman of the *Capital Times*. "You ask yourself, 'Where did you go wrong? What didn't we do? What can we do to make things right?'"

Donna's alleged killer had moved to another state. That didn't stop Rhodes. In the summer of '84, Rhodes and a fellow investigator traveled to the suspect's home hoping to discover the one piece of evidence needed to break open the case. They traveled back to Wisconsin with nothing.

"You've got to come up with some evidence," Rhodes said. "You can't work with a gut feeling."

Dick Josephson echoed Rhodes' point while reached by phone in 2021. While the unsolved Rothschild case was frustrating to him back in '68, he didn't have concrete evidence to bring a suspect to justice.

Marquette Slaying Sparks New Leads

Perhaps Donna's killer didn't stray too far from the grisly murder scene and had the penchant to strike again.

In July 1985, three years after the Mraz homicide shook the UW-Madison community, a very similar attack occurred at Marquette University, about an hour east of Madison. Around midnight, the same time Donna was stabbed, Antoinette Reardon, a twenty-year-old Marquette student, was attacked walking home from the Ardmore Bar, a popular hangout for college students. She was alone.

Reardon tried desperately to fight off her attacker. One fatal blow to the chest ended the struggle. The assailant ran off, leaving Reardon for dead. She struggled to get up, but was able to stagger down Wisconsin Avenue, leaving a stream of blood dripping onto the pavement. Around 12:15 a.m., two security guards from Marquette saw Reardon stumbling along the street and called for an ambulance.

Reardon died about three hours later at Milwaukee County Medical Complex. Meanwhile, police found Wilbert Wesley Jr., from Milwaukee, hiding in between two buildings near the crime scene. He was lying down, pretending to sleep. Wesley Jr. left the murder weapon, a blood-soaked knife, on a window ledge not far from where he attacked Reardon.

Reardon wasn't the killer's first potential victim. Police said Wesley Jr. approach another woman shortly before going after Reardon. Before she died, the Marquette student provided a few key details to detectives: "No, he didn't take anything from me. He didn't attempt to assault me. He didn't make any threats."

No sexual violence. No verbal threats. Appeared to be a totally random attack. Female college student. The case immediately piqued the interest of UW Police Chief Ralph Hanson. Could this be the guy who killed Donna Mraz?

The following day, Hanson sent two UW detectives to Milwaukee to investigate any possible connections. Twenty-eight-year-old Wesley Jr. was charged with first-degree murder. Bail was set at $105,000.

Similar to Mraz, Reardon had a bright, young life snuffed out by a crazed menace. A few hours before her attack, Reardon was enjoying a night out with friends. She had met up with a girlfriend for a few drinks at the Ardmore. Reardon and her friend left the tavern together but split up as Reardon approached her apartment. Wesley Jr. attacked and killed her one block from her home.

Reardon was from Kirkwood, Missouri, a suburb of St. Louis, but stayed in Milwaukee during the summer to work at Marquette University. She was studying biomedical engineering and was preparing to enter her senior year.

While the Reardon murder seemed like a carbon copy of the Mraz attack, UW police couldn't establish a true connection between both cases. Wesley Jr. was never charged with the murder of Donna Mraz.

Urge to Kill Doesn't Stop

It may seem unlikely the same man who killed Christine Rothschild on that cool, rainy morning in 1968 also murdered Mraz more than fourteen years later. For decades, however, the two perplexing cases have been linked together as the mysterious unsolved murders at the University of Wisconsin.

Forty years have passed since the horrific night Donna was killed in 1982 and, thanks to better security across campus, there hasn't been a fatal attack since. As the case lingered and the investigation stalled, there was a concern—at least in the initial years after Donna was murdered—that the killer could strike again.

"People who commit crimes like this don't just all of

a sudden stop," Chief Hanson told the *Capital Times*. "The urge they had to commit the crime is still with them."

In the summer of 1989, Balousek wrote an update on the Mraz case for the *State Journal*. "Update" should be taken loosely as very little new information was reported. But the veteran crime reporter's story kept the cold case in the public eye. By then, police had interviewed hundreds of possible witnesses and formed a decent description of the suspect: white, between twenty-five-to-thirty years old, five-foot-eight, and about one hundred and fifty pounds. His hair was straight and dark and he had a full beard. He wore a white T-shirt with green stripes and dark-colored pants.

Henry Lee Lucas, the convicted killer from Texas who was a suspect in the Bennett, Hall, Speerschneider, LeMahieu and Stewart cases, was briefly considered a suspect in the Mraz case. The way Donna was killed, however, didn't fit Lucas' M.O. of abducting and killing hitchhikers, then discarding the bodies in rural areas.

Shortly after the murder, the FBI pieced together a psychological profile of the killer. Investigators described him as an "emotionally immature would-be rapist who panicked when his intended victim resisted the assault." Neil Purtell, working as a special agent at the bureau's Madison office in 1982, said the profile was based on clues collected at the crime scene, including the time of the assault, how much force the killer used, and how much thought was put into the attack before it was committed.

The FBI believed the killer was several years younger than the person described by witnesses, possibly around eighteen or twenty years old. He felt comfortable lurking around under the cloak of darkness and likely lived near the crime scene, which could explain how he was able to escape from view so quickly. He was aware of his surroundings.

Purtell described the attack as a "blitz assault." He was probably afraid of Donna to begin with and when she resisted, he frantically scrambled to end it.

"He wanted to have absolute control over her," Purtell said in an interview with the *Capital Times*. "A guy like this is into a fantasy life. He doesn't have good interpersonal skills. Often, these people don't have girlfriends and if they have male friends, they will be younger than the offender."

The profile formulated a perverse picture of a young man addicted to pornography, socially stunted, and sexually immature. Often a "peeping tom," he is curious about women but would rather spy on them from afar rather than approach and engage in normal conversation. Fueled by several beers and hours of watching porn, the killer is emboldened. Booze and porn fill the deep, baseless cavern in his life. He's a wanderer. He decides to go for a walk. He needs to blow off steam, pent-up energy. He sees a pretty brunette, around his age, walking alone. It's his opportunity to strike.

"That's what I saw in this case," Purtell said. "Donna was in the wrong place at the wrong time and the offender was there."

Based on the investigation, the killer grabbed Donna from behind. She either never saw him coming or noticed at the last second. Still, Donna put up a fight, surprising the attacker. Typically, in those situations, according to the profile, the killer will flip a switch and respond with brute force. He's a coward. He needs to find some way to weasel out of the situation no matter what it costs. Even if that means taking a life.

The FBI believed the killer likely retreated back to his residence, perhaps a nearby apartment. A safe haven. But once the heat of the investigation boiled hotter, he ditched town and likely didn't return. Police were "getting too close," said Purtell.

Herb Hanson, a retired UW police detective, was one of the lead investigators on the Mraz case. When contacted for an interview in 2021, Hanson said he still remembers the case every July 2 as another anniversary passes. But he's been mostly removed from the cold case for decades and no longer considers himself a public source.

"Now, I just sit back in the shadows and reflect," Hanson said in an email.

Back in the early '80s, however, when Hanson was working long, tedious hours to find Donna's killer, he exhaustively picked through every lead.

"There wasn't one that wasn't followed up on," he told the *Capital Times.*

During the initial weeks after the murder, the Major Crime Unit worked day and night. They put together a list of suspects based off interviews with people who knew Donna. What baffled police even more was that the area Donna was attacked rarely saw violent crime. Detectives couldn't pinpoint typical criminals who hung around the stadium and Breese Terrace and pursue them.

"It was darn tough," said Frank McCoy, a former police detective from Madison who worked on the case for weeks. "There was a lot of shooting in the dark and grasping at straws. It was very frustrating."

In a 1992 interview with the newspaper, Hanson said, "We're as far away as the sun in solving this one, and as close as a phone call."

All UW detectives needed was someone to walk into the station and provide the missing piece to the puzzle.

"Somebody that night saw something, perhaps very innocently, and never associated it with this crime and it may be the piece that's desperately needed," Hanson said.

The Major Crime Unit, led by chief investigator Ron Tews from the UW police, was flooded with calls from tipsters, but none delivered a credible lead. People also sent suspicious knives they had found, thinking it could be the murder weapon. Also, the mysterious "bearded man" spotted walking around the stadium at about the time Donna was attacked was never found. Detectives would have loved to question him, but never got the chance. He wasn't pegged as a serious suspect.

Then there was the "bite-mark suspect." At the time of questioning, he was asked about the bite marks on his arm. He fluffed it off with a "bizarre answer," according to Hanson, but police didn't follow up on his odd reaction until months later. Perhaps in modern times, with DNA testing, results might be different but back in 1983, police couldn't match the bite from Donna to the suspect's injury.

While Ralph Hanson and FBI profilers felt confident the murder was a botched sexual assault, Herb Hanson couldn't draw that connection since there was no physical evidence of an attempted rape.

"There's no way I could even project that as the motive," Hanson told the *Capital Times*. "I couldn't draw that conclusion based on the scene and the evidence."

People kill, Hanson said. And in their warped minds, they don't always need a reason to do it.

For at least ten years after Donna was killed, detectives kept track of several suspects. It's unclear how much if any work still goes into the case forty years later as officials with UW police didn't specify when contacted in 2021.

"It disturbs me to this day that we don't know who did it," Tews said in 1992.

As much as it bothered the detectives that worked the case, for Donna's family it was pure torment. Lois Mraz, Donna's mother, told the *Capital Times* that investigators did all they could to find the murderer, but it couldn't take away her anguish. The shock of losing a child was one thing, having her death come at the hands of a killer was another, but the fact he could still walk the streets free and live a normal life ... at times was too difficult to bear.

The pain is always present.

"It never gets any easier," Mraz said. "It never changes. It just doesn't end."

In 1993, campus police set up the Crimestoppers tip line, replacing Campus Crime Watch, to help bring in information on the case. Since tipsters could remain anonymous and cash rewards were offered for valuable tips, it might lead to a crack in the decade-old cold case. Crimestoppers would also help keep Donna's murder in the public eye.

"Someone who wasn't willing to talk about it then may be willing to now," Sergeant Edie Brogan told the *State Journal*. "There is always human dynamics involved."

WKOW-TV Channel 27 in Madison filmed a reenactment of the case in early October 1993. As the years flew by and the case became colder by the decade, less interest was given to the Mraz murder. For detectives who worked closely on the case, like Herb Hanson, Donna's memory was never far away.

Hanson did an interview with *Capital Times* columnist Rob Zaleski for his "Up Close" column in the summer of 2004. The UW-Madison campus is typically a safe environment, but like many large universities, sexual assaults occur more often than the general public realizes. Throw in Wisconsin's high penchant for drinking and assaults are not uncommon. Random attacks, however, are rare but every once in a while, a violent encounter will make headlines.

Whenever an attack similar to the Mraz murder would make the news, Hanson would get chills. As one of the case's lead investigators, he recalled all too well that bloody crime scene in the summer of '82. In the column, Hanson noted another unsolved case. In '93, a twenty-six-year-old woman was stabbed multiple times by a crazed "knife-wielding" man who leapt from the shadows of the campus' Tripp-Adams residence hall. She survived but her attacker was never found.

While Madison is relatively safe, students can develop a naïve sense of comfort, thinking the campus is wrapped in a security blanket preventing any harm. For Donna, it was just like any other night when she walked off the bus near Camp Randall Stadium and started making her short trek home.

"I mean, who'd ever think somebody could get murdered walking outside Camp Randall Stadium on a July night?" Hanson said. "I'm sure Donna Mraz did not. But it happened."

Ned Pondry could relate. He was a student at UW-Madison shortly before Donna was killed. In the summer of 2009, the *Capital Times* ran a story on how investigators, despite being puzzled by few new leads, forged ahead to try to solve decades-old cold cases. Pondry penned a letter to the editor responding to the article.

> *The one I find especially disturbing is Donna Mraz, stabbed to death near Camp Randall Stadium in 1982, primarily because in the years 1978-1981 I was frequently on that end of campus ... When you imagine that something so horrible has happened in a place which you treated as a routine, almost subconscious path from class to home, or vice versa, never imagining there being any potential for violence–something like that is quite a shock. And the fact that there appear to be no leads, none. Zero.*

Hanson retired from the UW police force in 1997. His wife, Karen, was also a campus detective who worked on the case. The Mraz homicide was the most frustrating unsolved case of his career. Hanson realized, however, the frustration he felt not solving the murder paled in comparison to the staggering sense of loss Donna's family dealt with. That's why the Hansons made a point of calling her parents every July 2, the anniversary of their daughter's death.

"We just want to let them know we're thinking about them," Hanson told Zaleski.

Yet with so much time gone by, Hanson still felt in his gut the Mraz murder would one day be solved. The theory of a perfect crime doesn't exist, Hanson said. Especially in a homicide. It's too big of a situation for the killer to keep locked up inside himself for all that time.

"The perpetrator usually screws up one way or another," Hanson said. "They'll let something slip out while talking to somebody. Or they'll do something else that raises the level of suspicion."

Brother Grapples with Loss Decades Later

Mickey Mraz, Donna's only sibling, declined to be interviewed for this book, but he did grant one interview to NBC15 in Madison more than thirty-three years after he tragically lost his sister.

In the fall of 2015, the television station ran a news story blending an angle of recent cold cases being solved with the unsolved Mraz murder and steps the UW police have taken to improve campus security since Donna was attacked. While the story didn't provide any concrete updates on the case, it did shed light into who Donna really was and how the shocking murder affected her close friends and family. Mickey said Donna led a full life and showed a lot of promise.

"She was as busy as a bee, so she just got the nickname 'Buzzy,'" Mickey Mraz said in the interview.

He held an old black and white photo of Donna as

a young girl with her father standing beside her. Donna wore a white, checkered patterned dress with knee-high socks.

"She was daddy's little girl," Mickey said.

The hopes and dreams of Donna's parents were crushed on that dark night in 1982. UW Police Lieutenant Aaron Chapin, interviewed for the story, alluded to the killer having an almost animalistic rage when he attacked Donna.

"It's not normal for humans to want to do something like this to another human," said Chapin. "Specifically, something as brutal and as heinous as this case, you do take it a little personally that you can't get justice for the family."

As Mickey talked, grief washed over his face. Tears pooled in his eyes. More than three decades had passed since the night he found out his big sister had been murdered, but the memories never go away. The dark images stay locked somewhere in the back of the mind. The shocked look on his parents' faces. The anger. The deep, deep sadness. The years spent grieving a precious life taken way too soon. A senseless, tragic death. And ... *why?*

"You never forget the knock on the door," Mickey said. "And ... um ... the total turmoil in your life from that moment forth."

In the years following the Mraz murder, cameras were placed around campus. Security tightened. Donna was stabbed just outside the Gate 5 entrance to Camp Randall Stadium. Today, a camera would catch any similar type of attack and police could review the tape immediately.

Advancements in technology, combined with heightened security and awareness among students, has helped. It's been forty years since the last homicide on campus. Still, that leaves little solace to the Mraz family. In her report, NBC15 journalist Ashley Matthews said UW police considered the investigation "very open and active."

"Police are not giving up on this case," Matthews said.

However, that was back in 2015. Detectives working the case have either retired or moved on to other departments. There isn't much interest in the case currently, and with no new information flowing in and no credible leads to pursue, there isn't an urge by investigators to crack open the file.

Donna's case seems colder than ever.

"You totally can't live dwelling on it," Mickey said. "But it never goes away ... it's always there."

John Stofflet, co-anchoring the newscast that night, was a student at UW when Donna was killed. He recalled how the murder jolted the campus community. Stofflet led the segment with snippets of solved cold cases from southern Wisconsin. While Donna's unsolved case remains frustrating to many, there is hope. Breakthroughs in DNA forensic testing have been a game-changer, solving very dormant cold cases.

"As we've seen, some of the cases have been solved even decades later," Stofflet told co-anchor Leigh Mills.

But what if a critical error in judgement would prevent valuable evidence from being tested? What if the evidence had simply been thrown away?

Chapter 8

Genetic Testing Solves Wisconsin Cold Case

His neighbors were blown away by the news.

Ray from down the road? No, can't be him. A murderer? No way.

But it was all true. Ray Vannieuwenhoven, an eighty-two-year-old senior citizen living in the remote northeast Wisconsin town of Lakewood, brutally murdered two people. He lived with the crime for forty-three years until police used genetic genealogy to finally bring him to justice. In 2019, Vannieuwenhoven was arrested for the double murder of David Schuldes and fiancé Ellen Matheys in July 1976.

To Vannieuwenhoven's neighbors, he was a kind old man with an infectious laugh. He greeted everyone with a wave and a smile. The widower and father of five children mostly kept to himself in his modest ranch-style home in the woods of Marinette County. He had worked as a handyman and enjoyed helping people. But he lived with a dark secret for more than four decades.

On the afternoon of July 9, 1976, Schuldes and Matheys were settling in for a day of camping at McClintock Park, about twenty-five miles northeast from where Vannieuwenhoven was arrested decades later. They were planning to go for a walk when Matheys decided to use the restroom. Suddenly, two shots rang out, piercing this serene summer day. Her fiancé was shot in the neck and killed instantly. The assailant, blasting away from fifty feet, fired again and a bullet from his .30 caliber rifle stuck in the bathroom wall.

Matheys, terrified, ran for her life, but Vannieuwenhoven caught up to her. After raping her, he shot her twice in the chest. Police were puzzled to find a motive. Why this young couple? In the 1990s, as DNA testing became more reliable, local investigators sent semen collected from Mathey's shorts to a national FBI database. No matches came up.

In 2018, detectives tried another route. They sent the DNA evidence to Parabon Nanolabs, a company in Virginia specializing in genetic genealogy analysis. Since early 2018, the company has made headlines by helping solve cold cases from across the U.S. Parabon Nanolabs uploads DNA collected from long-dormant cases to GEDmatch, a genealogy database with millions of public profiles from people who've submitted their information to genealogy sites 23andMe and Ancestry.com.

That same year, the notorious Golden State Killer was finally nabbed through GEDmatch. Investigators found distant relatives and traced his family tree through a method called "reverse-engineering."

In the Vannieuwenhoven case, Parabon mapped

out his family tree in December 2018. They identified his parents who had lived around Green Bay. Detectives believed it was one of the Vannieuwehovens' four sons who committed the murders. They collected DNA samples, from collecting trash and testing a used coffee cup, from two of the brothers. On March 6, 2019, deputies from the Marinette County Sheriff's Department paid Ray Vannieuwenhoven a visit. They asked if he could fill out a short survey on the effects of local policing. When Vannieuwenhoven was done, they asked if he could place the survey in an envelope.

"If you could seal it up there with your tongue, that would be great," one of the two deputies asked.

Thinking nothing of it, Vannieuwenhoven sealed his fate.

About a week later, detectives arrived again at his house. This time it was not a friendly visit. There was no survey. Vannieuwenhoven was taken into custody for the murder of Matheys and Schuldes.

The alleged killer vehemently pleaded not guilty in court. Family members came to his defense, claiming he was a devoted family man, married to his wife Rita for more than fifty years. After she died in 2008, he lived a normal Wisconsin life, filled with hunting, fishing, and camping. Vannieuwenhoven, though, had brushes with the law in the past and showed patterns of violence. He was arrested as a young man in 1957 after attacking a seventeen-year-old girl. The girl was walking with three friends, minding her own business, when Vannieuwenhoven hit her on the face, shoulder and back. He apparently went out that day looking for violence. Not long before attacking the seventeen-year-old, Vannieuwenhoven tried going after another girl who was only sixteen.

He said he was only trying to scare the girls, but a judge sentenced him to six months in jail. A few years later, Vannieuwenhoven was placed on a year's long probation for not providing financial support to Rita and their one-year-old daughter.

Vannieuwenhoven also had a mean side when he drank. Fred Mason, who knew Vannieuwenhoeven for years, told the *Associated Press* that "he was one son of a bitch" after a few drinks. "You didn't want to be anywhere near him when he was drinking."

Yet, he kept a low profile and was known mostly as a friendly neighbor. That he committed such an awful crime rattled the sleepy Lakewood community.

"It's still hard to believe," one neighbor told the AP a few months after Vannieuwenhoven's arrest.

More than two years later, the families of Schuldes and Matheys finally received the justice they had waited decades for. On August 26, 2021, Vannieuwenhoven was sentenced to prison for two life sentences for the double homicide in 1976. Now eighty-four years old, the convicted killer faced his sentence sitting in a wheelchair looking pale and gaunt.

During sentencing, Marinette County Circuit Judge James Morrison spared no empathy for a sullen Vannieuwenhoven.

"This conduct was depraved in the worst sense ... The injuries to these two people, horrible," Morrison said, according to the Green Bay *Press-Gazette*. "The crimes, if there were a scale, would be a hundred on a scale of one-to-ten, when we talk about evil and damage, aggravated in every respect."

Schuldes' mother, ninety-three years old at the time of sentencing, did not appear in court, but told her daughter Jo-Anne Mikulsky, "I know it won't be over for me until he's in prison for the rest of his life." In her remaining years, she could finally have some closure knowing her son's and future daughter-in-law's killer was finally captured.

A second DNA test days after Vannieuwenhoven's arrest confirmed he left semen on Matheys' shorts. Still, his youngest daughter, Dorothy Vannieuwenhoven, refused to believe her father was a killer. She was the only person to speak on his behalf at the sentencing.

"The only thing you proved was that dad had an affair. I don't think you have the right guy," she said. "We all stood by you this whole time, not believing our dad could do anything like this, and I still believe that."

Since Vannieuwenhoven has never admitted to killing Matheys and Schuldes, it may never be known why he targeted a happy, young couple he apparently didn't know. Similar to Mraz, they were likely chosen at random.

Two more promising lives ended in an act of senseless violence.

"To pick out two kids in a half an hour of opportunity and end their lives, terminate their hopes, cause grievous harm to their family and friends ... I do not have words to describe how horrible this is," Judge Morrison said.

Many cases from the '70s and even older have been solved due to DNA evidence testing. It's a major breakthrough in science and criminology that's finally put to bed cold cases deemed unsolvable.

Could that bring hope to the families of the seven young women featured in this book?

In some of the cases, where bodies had been left in remote, wooded areas, there wasn't a lot of evidence left to collect. However, in cases like Rothschild's, there was ample evidence taken at the scene. As these cases lingered, materials were locked away in evidence rooms for years, not to be touched until a case could be reopened.

Unless someone decided to say ... throw them out. Discard them. Destroy them.

The potential to solve these cases—even with DNA testing—just became a lot more difficult.

Chapter 9

Mistakes Lead to Lost Evidence

No one wanted to admit to it, for good reason.

Somehow, in the shuffle and haste of moving to another building, evidence in open cases was discarded by the Dane County Sheriff's Office sometime in the late 1980s. The mistake was forgotten about until a concerned whistleblower—a former sheriff's office employee—provided a tip to the *Capital Times*.

Headlined: "LOST IN THE SHUFFLE. Police have thrown out or lost evidence in at least four Dane County cold cases." The story was bound to stop readers in their tracks. *How? Why?*

Capital Times reporter Steven Elbow investigated the lead and dived into months of research and interviews. He found that out of ten cold case homicides being investigated by the sheriff's office, Madison Police Department and UW police, "at least four have been compromised by the mishandling of evidence."

Three of those cases were the murders of Christine

Rothschild, Julie Speerschneider, and Shirley Stewart. Specifically, Elbow was looking into the Stewart, Speerschneider, Julie Hall and Debra Bennett cases.

"The first thing I did was put out a request (for information) out to the sheriff's department and the Madison Police Department," Elbow said in a 2021 phone interview. "That's how I found out about (Mark) Justl."

In the early morning hours of November 22, 1972, Justl, a young Madison resident, was beaten to death. Only seven months later, valuable evidence taken from the scene was destroyed, including clothing, blood, pieces of hair, cigarette butts... all items that likely had DNA evidence. Elbow interviewed Justl's ninety-five-year-old mother for the story in 2010. Genevieve Justl always wondered why her son's case was literally doomed from the start.

Through his records request, Elbow received many police reports, handwritten back in the '70s.

"I had all these hand-written notes and within that was something about destroying evidence," Elbow said. "That was in the police report, too. So that was on paper. It was something I got back from them, and all the information was there.

"The Justl case is a pretty blatant example of evidence getting destroyed."

Roger Attoe, a detective who signed off on throwing away the evidence, could provide Justl's mother with no explanation. Attoe died in 2007. Charles Lulling, the first lead detective on the Justl case and an investigator who also worked on the Rothschild case, died back in 2000.

For his story, Elbow talked to Steve Reinstra, a retired Madison police detective who was baffled that evidence was thrown out. He spent time working on the Justl case in the mid-2000s.

"I'm not sure why the evidence was disposed of," Reinstra said. "We could have gotten some DNA off of some of that stuff. It's too bad."

While its odd and frustrating evidence in open cases, including sexual assaults and vehicular homicides, was destroyed, it's tough to blame the officers who tossed the materials. They were simply following orders from superiors.

"There was a big push by our bosses to get everything out of there," Reinstra told Elbow. "They would give us these property tags and say, 'You look at this and you get rid of it. We need to clean out the property room.' Unfortunately, some of those things should have been prioritized."

Part of the problem was the sheriff's department, by the mid-1980s, was running out of space. The property room at the City-County Building in downtown Madison was cramped. Detectives felt some evidence needed to be purged to make room for new materials. But which cases took priority over others? Isn't one unsolved murder just as important as the next one?

According to Reinstra, some old cases were finally being solved because evidence in that property room was saved.

"Some departments were very protective of that evidence, and they had plenty of room to store it," Reinstra said.

In 1988, the sheriff's department renovated one of its rooms at the City-County Building to create more space for property, but in the process, the agency made the mistake of throwing out physical evidence in two active murder cases, according to Elbow.

The tip from the former department employee to the *Capital Times* led the paper to inquire about the lost evidence, which pushed the sheriff's office to launch an internal review. The findings were startling. In both the Shirley Stewart and Julie Speerschneider cases, "nearly all evidence has been destroyed." In the Christine Rothschild case, the first high-profile murder to be investigated by the Intra-County Task Force, vital evidence had vanished. It's possible, since three departments, UW police, Madison Police, and the sheriff's department, all worked on the 1968 homicide, that materials were mishandled in the back-and-forth shuffle between agencies.

In the late '60s, campus police didn't yet have a room to store evidence. All materials collected from the scene of the Rothschild murder were stored at the sheriff's department. In 2007, Sue Riseling was chief of the UW police. Riseling decided to take a fresh look at the Rothschild case. She instructed an investigative team to track down all evidence from a nearly forty-year-old cold case. One problem. It was not preserved the way Riseling figured it would be by the sheriff's department.

Evidence sent to the FBI in Washington days after the murder was tested and shipped back to Madison. However, records of what was done with the evidence were simply lost. Riseling requested the sheriff's office to look through its property room for several years to locate what was missing.

"Obviously, that didn't happen," Riseling said in the

Capital Times story. "And then with this review, since they've really gone through everything thoroughly, it doesn't look like it's going to happen."

While there was still some evidence in the Rothschild case intact as of 2010, Riseling admitted solving the case became even more daunting with items unavailable for DNA testing.

Who Authorized It?

"I don't know if they even know who lost it," Elbow said in 2021. "The main dynamic was that the sheriff's department didn't want to give me any information. And they were really kind of shitty about it. When they did their review, they wouldn't give me anything on paper, they wouldn't do a phone interview. They ended up calling me in."

After stalling to provide information through open records requests, the *Capital Times* was prepared to file a lawsuit against the sheriff's department. That's when the agency tried to turn the tables. In a strange encounter that Elbow claims was a strong-armed intimidation tactic, Sheriff Dave Mahoney, along with Deputy Sheriff Jeff Hook, brought Elbow into a room with several detectives.

"They sat at the table and told me what a shitty person I was for trying to get this information on active cases," Elbow said.

Looking back a decade later, Mahoney was surprised to hear Elbow felt intimidated during the interview. He admits he should have taken a lighter approach to the newspaper's investigation, but he was also standing up for his department.

"Maybe I should have toned it down a little," Mahoney

said in a 2022 interview. "But I know Steven and to this day, I don't have any animosity toward him, or any member of the media. I might have been defensive. But I don't really remember much from the meeting. I do remember the story and the process of working on the story."

The retired sheriff said he always tried to be transparent and honest with the media and the public, but there were times when he had to "minimalize" information to protect the integrity of an investigation. In the *Cap Times'* probe, the department eventually relented and showed Elbow the results of its internal investigation. It wasn't good.

"They lost a whole bunch of evidence that could have been used—a lot of potential DNA evidence—and they were pretty embarrassed about it," Elbow said. "That was the last thing I had to do for this story, meeting with them because they took so long.

"The whole unraveling of this story took months. I put it on the backburner. Put in open records requests in whenever I would think to do it. Then the sheriff's department launched an investigation into their own practices. I'm glad I waited until they released that because that was a major element of the story."

Despite the tension in the room, once Elbow sat down with department officials, they gave him as much information as they had to.

"I don't think they gave me the internal report; everything they gave me was verbally," Elbow said. "We chose not to sue to get the internal report. I think we figured we had enough, and we knew they had already investigated themselves on the premise that they lost all this evidence."

The original whistleblower to the lost evidence, who requested anonymity, told Elbow that in the late '80s, Lieutenant Larry Lathrop, who supervised the sheriff department's evidence room, told staff to dispose of evidence to make room in the crowded facility. The informant claimed it was a "widespread purge," but Mahoney, who retired as sheriff in 2021, claimed the evidence dump never happened. Lou Molnar, a former evidence technician with the department, disputed Mahoney's denial.

"They probably wouldn't have given us anything but if we had gotten a lawyer, they would have had to because it's all stuff that they had to release," Elbow said.

Lathrop also denied Molnar's claim that he ordered the evidence purge in an email to the *Capital Times*.

"I would not have had the authority to authorize the destruction of evidence, nor would your sources have been authorized to destroy said evidence with only my authorization."

The sheriff's department told the *Capital Times* Lathrop didn't take over the evidence room until 1992, a few years after it's believed the evidence was destroyed. Mahoney told Elbow the former lieutenant was off the hook via the department's investigation.

In 2022, Mahoney said there could have been a host of reasons why the evidence was disposed of.

"Some of it is accidental loss of evidence or contamination; a lot of these cases were contamination," Mahoney said. "The (evidence) wasn't quite dried long enough, they were packaged up and twenty years later, you open up the bag and it's full of mold. There's not much you can do but throw it out. And then, some of it is haphazard maintenance ... some of it is laziness where it's a fifty-year-old case and someone clearing the evidence room at the time said, 'This isn't that important.'"

Captain Tim Ritter, who oversaw the evidence room back in 2010, told Elbow during the tense meeting that while there were items related to those open cases destroyed in the purge, Ritter said it was "not a great deal" of evidence. Mahoney, meanwhile, claimed there was still "substantial evidence" remaining from those cases.

The sheriff's office changed its tune dramatically, however, about a week before Elbow's piece hit the newsstands.

In a huge revelation, a panel of sheriff's officials admitted that parts of Speerschneider's skeletal remains were discarded in 1981, while a gold hoop earring she was wearing was also disposed of in the fall of 1988. In 1993, other documents pertaining to the Speerschneider case from 1981 were thrown out.

Even more troubling, in the Shirley Stewart case, it was found that several items were destroyed. Her skeletal remains were sent to a funeral home, but the date was never determined. Police also retrieved a twelve-gauge shotgun shell, but believed at the time it was not connected to the case, so it was discarded. In October 1988—the same month evidence from the Speerschneider case was tossed—hair found at the base of Stewart's skull, a Timex watch and a bra were all disposed of.

One careless decision wiped out all the remaining evidence in the Stewart case. The Speerschneider case wasn't as damaged, but the only remaining items as of

2010 were interviews recorded on video. All physical evidence was gone.

"They lost all that stuff," Elbow said.

Vital physical evidence that could have been tested for DNA years later. The alleged dumping of evidence occurred in the late '80s. While DNA testing wouldn't really amp up in police investigations until several years later, it baffled Elbow that any evidence in open cases would be considered not worthy of retaining. Especially since Mahoney and Ritter stressed in their interview that the sheriff's department sporadically reviews aging cold cases.

"The big thing was the lost evidence; it was just handled differently," Elbow said. "And the documents from the Madison police in particular that explicitly said what happened. Somebody ordered all the evidence in this case destroyed and it got destroyed."

In the department's internal review, Lieutenant Tim Schuetz from the professional standards office led the inquiry into what happened with the Stewart and Speerschneider cases. Schuetz found the two former department employees who signed off on the evidence disposal, Lieutenant Steve Gilmore, responsible for the 1988 evidence disposal, and lab technician Shawn Haney, who reportedly approved the 1993 shredding of documents in the Speerschneider homicide.

Elbow attempted to reach Gilmore for an interview, but never connected with him. Schuetz, however, said Gilmore signed off on the evidence destruction because the sheriff's office was planning to expand the City-County Building's evidence room.

Haney was reached by phone and told Elbow while he

didn't specifically remember what documents were tossed, he claimed the disposal occurred when the department was preparing to move from the City-County Building to the Public Safety Building between 1992 and 1994. In the Speerschneider case, Haney thought documents were somehow moved away from other evidence and placed in a "document drawer."

"There's a possibility that it got looked at and someone said, 'Well this doesn't have any real relevance to the case,' and it got destroyed," Haney told Elbow. "That's the best we can think of, because we wouldn't knowingly destroy evidence in an active homicide case."

In more recent years, perhaps because of such mishaps, law enforcement departments have stricter procedures to guard against throwing away valuable evidence. While retaining evidence was looser in the 1980s and '90s, Schuetz said there were still security measures in place that were clearly not followed.

As part of the internal investigation, Haney provided Schuetz with written explanations of why the evidence was thrown out. He described the evidence room back in the early '90s as "a mess."

Haney wrote: "We just started with each shelf, made a list and started checking to see if cases were active or closed. If the cases were closed, we disposed of the property in accordance with what we were told by the detective, DA's office, etc."

Mahoney said evidence stored in packages from decades ago often became contaminated with mold and other chemicals simply from sitting in evidence rooms for many years. He said evidence was likely thrown out because it was basically ruined from decomposition.

"Unfortunately, in a number of our homicide cases, evidence became deteriorated or, unbeknownst to us, the evidence became contaminated with water/mildew and then we have no DNA evidence," Mahoney said. "For instance, if we had a piece of bloody clothing, we would air dry it and then package it up. Back then, we had no idea that years later, there would be these advancements in DNA that we could analyze that blood to possibly identify a suspect. When case detectives review these cases, those are the type of things they're keeping an eye on, whether it was DNA evidence, even familial DNA evidence. Most recently, 23andMe and Ancestry.com is being used to identify these suspects and that's how a lot of these old homicides are being solved."

Having covered crime for the Portage (Wisconsin) *Daily Register* in the 1990s, Elbow was familiar with evidence rooms. Many were a mess. Before the digital age ushered in new ways to catalog materials, busy police departments stashed evidence wherever they could.

"It was a place where people piled bags full of crap," Elbow said. "I've walked into them before, and I've seen open pot plants just sitting there."

Even food was left out, including that of one of America's most notorious serial killers.

"In Columbia County, I saw the remains of Jeffrey Dahmer's last dinner in a paper bag in the refrigerator," Elbow said. "It's like, 'What is that doing there?'"

As evidence accumulated and cases remained open,

departments had a difficult time keeping track of what's what, especially as space became limited.

"They were just not good at keeping track of stuff so they would have these occasional purges," Elbow said. "Now a lot of it is stored digitally, at least what can be stored digitally. They can take pictures. There are new refrigerators to store blood samples and things to keep evidence intact better than what they used to. It's just a different world."

Mahoney agreed, saying when he started his law enforcement career in 1980, evidence was often stored haphazardly.

"Back then, true evidence rooms—compared to the standards of today—were virtually nonexistent," Mahoney said. "You might have had an evidence locker where an evidence technician would put all his evidence in that locker. So, you would have three or four homicides stored away in that one locker."

Packing evidence into one locker sometimes led to missing pieces, such as evidence tags that could have fallen off, making it difficult to identify which evidence belongs to what case years down the road. In the early '80s, Mahoney said officers would simply grab a paper grocery bag, plop evidence in, staple it shut, and mark what evidence it contained on the outside with a black marker, along with the case number.

"You could have multiple bags with no tags and multiple tags just sitting on the floor," Mahoney said. "They might have been just stapled or taped on and fell off. As the years moved along, things changed. Now we use bar coding ... it's more computerized and a lot more professional. There's a record kept of every piece of evidence."

To safeguard against valuable evidence being lost or destroyed, Mahoney said the sheriff's department implemented a policy in recent years in which at least three supervisors must sign off on whether a piece of evidence gets discarded.

"You got the evidence room technician who is maintaining and determining what evidence can be destroyed and then they make a recommendation to their supervisor; their supervisor then has to get approval from their commander, so there's three opportunities to catch a mistake, either intentional or inadvertent," Mahoney said. "Today, what might seem like an inconsequential piece of evidence might be valuable twenty-five years from now. We just don't know what will happen with technology. Maybe they'll develop some technology to separate mold from DNA. Really with mold, you have the potential where it can contaminate other evidence–then what are you going to do?"

DNA testing to solve cold cases has also come a long way since the 1980s. About two decades ago, police still needed blood the size of a quarter to get a strong DNA sample. By the early 2010s, however, detectives could snag a viable sample from the top of a soda can a suspect had sipped on, fingerprints, and in the case of Ray Vannieuwenhoven, a licked envelope.

The FBI formed the Combined DNA Index System in 1990, a storage base of samples from state, local, and federal crime labs. Investigators can search for matches through the system. While the technology has led to many stagnant cases being reopened with fresh leads and new suspects, it's also helped exonerate many criminals falsely convicted and sent to prison for violent crimes.

Closer to Madison, DNA evidence has led to the convictions of Edward Edwards for the 1980 double murder of Timothy Hack and Kelly Drew in Jefferson County, and Curtis Forbes finally being brought to justice for the killing of Marilyn McIntyre, a young mother living in Columbus, also in 1980.

The success of solving cases through DNA led to local departments receiving state and federal grants to pursue old, unsolved homicides, such as the Madison Police Department's reopening of the Speerschneider case in 2015. DNA testing, though, is a non-starter if the evidence isn't there to be tested.

"It's difficult to use the advances of forensic science if you have nothing to apply it to," Madison Police Department Captain Jay Lengfeld told the *Capital Times*.

That makes solving cases like Christine Rothschild's, Shirley Stewart's and Julie Speerschneider's almost impossible, unless someone finally comes forward with new information.

"It would likely take a confession or for somebody that was close enough (to the crime) to be able to talk about what happened," Elbow said. "That's about all that's left. And, every year that passes, whoever did it, it's increasingly likely they're dead."

Conclusion

Imagine carrying a deep, dark secret for more than forty years. Or, in the case of Christine Rothschild, for more than five decades.

What goes through the mind of a murderer? Are they constantly haunted by the memories of their brutal act or does it matter little to them? Do they have a conscious? Do they possess any remorse?

These are the burning questions the killers of Christine Rothschild, Debra Bennett, Julie Hall, Julie Speerschneider, Susan LeMahieu, Shirley Stewart, and Donna Mraz must answer to. But are they still around to face justice? Will they or have they already gone to their graves knowing they took a precious life away from the people they loved? If they are still alive, will they ever confess?

As an avid true crime follower and journalist, I've always been fascinated by how killers can live their lives knowing they committed a heinous act. If they're delusional, and feel as if they've done nothing wrong, they likely feel no guilt. Perhaps they believe they're innocent and feel no desire to face justice. Others may enjoy the powerful, domineering effect they have on women and believe their victims "had it coming." They're not steeped in reality and have no basis of common sense.

In a couple of the cases profiled here, those responsible for the murders might feel the death was accidental. They could have panicked knowing the victim was deceased. In their haste, they might have burned the body or discarded the young woman in a wooded area figuring their deadly mistake will be hidden for some time, maybe forever. They've remained frightened to approach the police for decades knowing what the consequences could be.

Then there are those who simply have a burning desire to kill. These are the darkest members of society. The need to fulfill their evil urges overpowers them to the brink. They must lash out. Perhaps Henry Lee Lucas fits this description. He "confessed" to hundreds of murders and eventually recanted on most of them. Was his goal to be infamous? Did he want to be labeled as the nation's most notorious serial killer? Lucas died many years ago, so it's likely we'll never know the real answer. And that's maybe the most maddening reason men like Lucas commit murders–notoriety. Making headlines. Evading police. Constantly running with secrets. Killing again if they had the chance.

Avoiding capture forever.

Whether tormented or not, the murderers of the seven young women I wrote about went on to live their lives. The victims did not. Their family and friends got to keep living, but what kind of life did they lead after their loved one was murdered? Depression took over for some, while others, such as Christine Rothschild's parents, kept the painful memories bottled up, never speaking of her again. Julie Speerschneider's family faces the constant reminders when another woman goes missing and the press digs up archived blurbs about their sister's cold case. Susan LeMahieu's siblings, on the other hand, choose to reflect on the good memories of Sue's life–her kindness, her independent spirit–rather than the tragic way she died.

How family and friends grapple with a loved one being murdered can be very complex. There's a wide range of emotions and for some, traumatically deep scarring that lasts a lifetime. As Mickey Mraz, the younger brother of Donna Mraz put it, "You never really get over it." Combining the shock of murder with the realization their case may never be solved is even more difficult to grasp.

Murder, especially unsolved cases, tends to cause a ripple effect going beyond immediate family. Cousins, nieces, and nephews are affected. Roommates, close friends, boyfriends, and acquaintances are impacted. Teachers, professors, mentors, co-workers, and bosses feel the pain and anguish. In addition, the investigators that have spent years trying to solve these baffling cases are also emotionally invested. These are the cases they never forget. A few of the women I wrote about grew up in small towns where unsolved homicides tend to vibrate throughout close-knit Wisconsin communities.

Hopefully, I was able to shed light on these murder victims that seem forgotten to the general public, but are often on the minds of the close family and friends they left behind. If this book leads to a break in any of these cases, I would be ecstatic, but if not, at least it's getting these important cases back in the public realm. To borrow the theme from "Unsolved Mysteries" host Robert Stack, someone, somewhere knows something. Someone walking amongst us in everyday life likely has vital information to help solve these cases.

Heeding veteran journalist George Hesselberg's words of wisdom, I didn't go about this project to solve any of these cases, but I'm hoping that you, the reader, have a better understanding of all of them. Not only the details and circumstances surrounding the murders, but also the complexities as to why they've gone unsolved for decades.

More importantly, I hope I've done enough to share the stories of these seven young women. Hopefully, you've gotten to know them as persons, not just victims of unsolved homicides. Because they're more than just numbers or statistics, they're sisters, girlfriends, best friends, daughters, cousins, and in the case of Shirley Stewart, mothers. They all left their impact on this world. Their deaths leave a huge void that can never truly be filled.

If you have any information about these unsolved murders, please contact the Dane County Sheriff's Office at 608-284-6800; the Madison Police Department, 608-255-2345 or the UW-Madison Police Department, 608-264-2677.

ACKNOWLEDGMENTS

Writing a book is an arduous task. At times it can feel daunting, lonely, frustrating, and so many more emotions, but in the end it's completely worth it.

And, considering this is my first book project, I really didn't know what to expect when I jumped into working on it almost three years ago. But the work you're holding in your hands could not have been completed without the help of many caring friends, family, colleagues and trusted sources.

First, the sources. Thank you to retired journalist and author Marv Balousek. I thoroughly enjoyed meeting with you over Zoom. Your expertise on these cases and memories of covering them were invaluable to this project. I hope you're enjoying retirement in Florida and still covering those village board meetings when the journalism bug hits.

Thanks to Steve Elbow of the *Capital Times*. Your 2010 piece of investigative journalism was excellent, and it provided an amazing (albeit frustrating) plot twist to some of the cases I've covered. Thank you for taking the time to go over how the story unfolded and the process of retrieving valuable information. Steve, you're a dogged reporter and your willingness to dig for information was an inspiration as I continued to dive into these stories.

George Hesselberg, retired journalist, thanks for your insight and valuable advice.

To all of the retired and active law enforcement personnel I talked to—thank you, thank you, thank you! This project would not have been worth its salt without your input.

Special thanks to retired Dane County Sheriff Dave Mahoney. I appreciated your honesty and willingness to discuss the lost evidence. Your expertise and years of policing really helped uncover many questions. I'll never forget seeing you tear up discussing how meaningful it was to finally solve the homicide of a young girl in Dane County. I could tell you brought a level of heart and compassion to your job and there's no doubt you're missed at the Dane County Sheriff's Office. Next time we meet up, the coffee is on me.

Mike Hanson, captain with the Madison Police Department, thank you so much for welcoming me into your office. It was fun hearing all the wonderful memories of your father and seeing his amazing artwork. Through my reporting and our discussion, your father's desire to solve the Christine Rothschild and Donna Mraz murders was purely evident. He didn't get to see you follow in his footsteps, but I'm sure he would be extremely proud.

Linda Schulko, you penned a pretty damn good book of your own, trying to solve the mystery of your friend's shocking murder. Thank you so much for your time and memories of Christine. You only knew her for a short time but her impact on your life has lasted more than fifty years. Keep fighting and advocating for your dear friend.

Thanks to retired detectives Herb Hanson and Dick

Josephson for their memories of the Rothschild and Mraz homicides. Retired Det. Rick Luell from the Wisconsin Department of Justice, your reflection on the Rothschild case was key in helping put the puzzle together and open my mind to other suspects. Det. Dan Nale, thank you for looking back on the reopening of the Julie Speerschneider case and being as open and transparent as you could.

Thanks to family members of the victims who provided insight into their lost loved ones, including Marcia Schiffman and the family of Sue LeMahieu.

Gratitude also goes out to members of the Madison Police Department, Dane County Sheriff's Office, and the University of Wisconsin Police Department for assistance.

Newspapers.com was a HUGE help in researching these decades old cases. In a matter of seconds, I could log on, type in a search, and dozens of archived stories popped up. Speaking of which, I leaned heavily on reporting from the *Wisconsin State Journal* and *Capital Times*. Both Madison newspapers covered these cases extensively and the journalism that unfolded on those pages opened a door to the past, not just on the dynamics of the cases, but on the lives of these young women. Special thanks to the reporters who steadfastly covered these cases decades ago.

Thanks to Mirin Fader and Jeff Pearlman, both big-time authors and outstanding journalists, for their shots of timely feedback and encouragement.

Very special gratitude goes out to Kira Moericke, my manuscript editor, for her sharp eye and attention to detail. So thankful you took on this project. Kira, your career is just getting off the ground but you have a bright future in writing and editing. Hope we can work together again sometime.

Also, thanks to friend and former newspaper colleague Mark McMullen for providing a thorough proof of the book.

Thanks to Jason Cuevas, former boss and editor from my Capital Newspapers days. You encouraged me to pursue the cold case feature story back in 2017, which won an award and helped kickstart this project.

Special thanks to Christine Keleny for her excellent work on redesigning the book from it's original format.

Shout out to my current colleagues at the Department of Veterans Affairs and the My Life, My Story program: Thor Ringler, Seth Jovaag, Lauren Koshere and Jane Barbian. I was a bit apprehensive when I decided to leap out of journalism and into the narrative storytelling/mental health field, but what a good decision! I couldn't have asked for a kinder, more intelligent, talented and passionate group to work with. We are small but we are mighty.

To my parents, Nancy and my later father, Bert. Thank you for nurturing my love for writing and storytelling at an early age. Tip of the hat also to my brother Don for his support through the years.

Genuine love and appreciation to all my friends on social media who responded with excitement when I reported I was about a quarter-way through writing my first book. Your enthusiasm and curiousness helped push me through all those difficult days when I didn't think I could keep going.

Of course, thank you to my wife, Jenny. You encouraged me to follow my dream of writing a book ... and about three-quarters of the way through you probably regretted it, haha. Thank you so much for your patience and understanding, along with editing help, feedback and guidance. Love you to the moon and back.

Finally, special thanks to my son, Jackson. I pressed pause on all of this work when you arrived in the fall of 2021 but I'm so glad you're here. It'll be a while before you read this but I hope, one day, you'll pick up this book and think of me with a little sense of pride because I couldn't be prouder to be your dad. Love you, buddy.

Notes

While several interviews were conducted and used as primary sources (as noted in the book), the author primarily used newspaper and online articles, along with television news reports for source material.

Chapter 1

Christine Rothschild

Dave Zweifel, "Police Search for Clues in UW Slaying," Capital Times, May 27, 1968

Whitney Gould, "Christine: She Had Smile for Everybody," Capital Times, May 27, 1968

William Granger, "Co-Ed From Chicago Slain, 18-Year-Old is Killed at Wisconsin U," Chicago Tribune, May 27, 1968

Staff, "3 Youths Beat Man Who Tries To Protect His Wife, In 600 Block of University Avenue," Capital Times, May 27, 1968

Staff, (Map/photo), "Where the Slain Co-ed Was Found," Capital Times, May 27, 1968

Robert Joslyn, "40 Mugging Cases Spur Action Here," Wisconsin State Journal, May 28, 1968

Staff, "Candidate's Statement: Sen. Warren Ties Campus Slaying and Lawlessness," Capital Times, May 28, 1968

Owen Coyle, "Hanson Says No New Leads Yet, Also Ask U. Doctor To Assist," Capital Times, May 28, 1968

Robert Nolte, "Police Seek Student Help In Co-Ed Death," Chicago Tribune, May 28, 1968

Patricia Krizmis, "'Everything She Touched Was Success,' Says Co-ed's Mother," Chicago Tribune, May 28, 1968

Robert Nolte, "Officials Hint Link to Percy Case, Find Trousers Near Scene of Co-ed Slaying," Chicago Tribune, May 28, 1968

Staff, "A Happy Life Ends for Well-Liked Girl, Why Her? Friends Ask," Wisconsin State Journal, May 28, 1968

June Dieckmann, "No Clue Found in UW Slaying, Autopsy Reveals Stabbing, Blows," Wisconsin State Journal, May 28, 1968

Robert Nolte, "Eye Another Student in Slaying of Co-ed," Chicago Tribune, May 29, 1968

Dave Zweifel, "Trousers, Knife Studied In Campus Murder Probe," Capital Times, May 29, 1968

June Dieckmann, "Two Clues Studied in Co-ed Murder," Wisconsin State Journal, May 29, 1968

Staff editorial, "The Murder at the University: Were There Witnesses?" Wisconsin State Journal, May 29, 1968

Staff, "Larger Police Force Eyed for UW Campus," Wisconsin State Journal, May 29, 1968

Dave Zweifel, "Tired Police Continue the Search for Murder Clues, No Leads in Co-ed's Slaying," Capital Times, May 30, 1968

Robert Nolte, "Police to Quiz Student, 19, in Co-ed Slaying," Chicago Tribune, May 30, 1968

Marvin Levy, "Meeting Bares Gap Between Students, Police," Wisconsin State Journal, May 30, 1968

June Dieckmann, "Police Look for a Break in Co-ed Case," Wisconsin State Journal, May 30, 1968

Staff editorial, "Sen. Warren Tries to Milk Votes from Rothschild Tragedy," Capital Times, May 30, 1968

Staff, "No Suspects, No One held in Co-ed Case," Wisconsin State Journal, May 31, 1968

Dave Zweifel, "Psychiatrist Reports: Sees Wide Range In Type of Killer," Capital Times, May 31, 1968

Robert Nolte, "End Violence, Madison Urges," Chicago Tribune, June 1, 1968

Staff, "Hanson Mum on Co-ed Slaying," Wisconsin State Journal, June 2, 1968

Staff, "Police Report No Clew in Co-ed Murder," Chicago Tribune, June 3, 1968

Irvin Kreisman, "City Man Is Murder Suspect, Has Long Problem History," Wisconsin State Journal, June 4, 1968

Richard Brautigam, "Mayor's Group Says City Must End Street Attacks, Hears Stories of Assaults on Students," Capital Times, June 4, 1968

Jon Wegge, "Campaign Urged on Street Crime, With City-UW Cooperation," Wisconsin State Journal," June 4, 1968

Staff, "Quiz Mental Patient in Slaying of Co-ed," Chicago Tribune, June 4, 1968

June Dieckmann, "$5,000 Reward for UW Slayer, Campus Chief Asks for Funds," Wisconsin State Journal, June 4, 1968

Irvin Kreisman, "Police Study Reports; Still Hunt Knife," Capital Times, June 5, 1968

June Dieckmann, "Three Leads in Co-ed Slaying at UW Fade," Wisconsin State Journal, June 5, 1968

Staff, "Quiz Mental Patient Again in Co-ed Death," Chicago Tribune, June 5, 1968

Staff, "Probers Find No South Hall Fire Suspects," Wisconsin State Journal, June 5, 1968

Staff, "Leslie Versus Crime Lab," Capital Times, June 5, 1968

Staff, "Lack of Clues Stymies Probe of Co-ed Death," Wisconsin State Journal, June 6, 1968

Staff, "50 Lawmen Plan Hunt for Knife That Killed Co-ed," Wisconsin State Journal, June 12, 1968

Roger Gribble, "'Beefed-Up' UW Police May Get Even Stronger, Additional State Funds Eyed" Wisconsin State Journal, June 14, 1968

Staff, "Reward Upped in Co-ed Case," Wisconsin State Journal, June 15, 1968

June Dieckmann, "Christine's Killer Still Sought – 4 Weeks Later," Wisconsin State Journal, June 23, 1968

Staff, "Madison Crimes Climb 35% So Far This Year, Campus Killing Not 'In City,"' – Capital Times, June 25, 1968

Staff, "Police Are Baffled in Coed's Murder," Wisconsin State Journal, June 25, 1968

Irvin Kreisman, "Is Probe of Campus Murder Floundering? Veteran Police Reporter Irvin Kreisman Reviews Case After A Month," Capital Times, June 26, 1968

Irvin Kreisman, "Police Sketch 'Recreates Campus

Killer,' Based on Descriptions of Two Co-ed Attack Victims," Capital Times, July 3, 1968

Staff (photo/cutline), "Is This the Killer," Capital Times, July 3, 1968

Staff, "Release Sketch of Suspect in Chicago Co-ed's Death," Chicago Tribune, July 3, 1968

June Dieckmann, "Police Seek Sketch Suspect in Rothschild Murder Case," Wisconsin State Journal, July 4, 1968

Staff, "Switchblade Is Found; Seek Murder Link," Capital Times, July 4, 1968

Irvin Kreisman, "Ex-Convict's Picture Has Resemblance To Death Suspect Sketch, Suspect Has Long Sex Crime Record," Capital Times, July 5, 1968

Staff, "Seek Link in Ann Arbor, Chicago and U.W. Slayings," Capital Times, July 10, 1968

Staff, "Big 10 Police Check Slaying of UW Co-ed," Wisconsin State Journal, July 11, 1968

Staff, "Officers Feud Revealed," Capital Times, July 24, 1968

June Dieckmann, "Molester Grabs Six Co-eds, Police Seek Grinning Suspect," Wisconsin State Journal, July 25, 1968

Irvin Kreisman, "U. Police To Start Night Foot Patrols, Will Establish Sub-Station," Capital Times, Sept. 5, 1968

Staff, "Madison Cops Search in Detroit, N.Y." Chicago Tribune, Sept. 17, 1968

Staff, "Doctor Wanted for Questioning in Co-ed Murder," Wisconsin State Journal, Sept. 18, 1968

Irvin Kreisman, "Quizzed 4 Hrs. In New York, Denies

Knowledge of Rothschild Case," Capital Times, Sept. 19, 1968

Staff, "Doctor to Be Quizzed Anew in Death Probe," Capital Times, Sept. 20, 1968

Staff, "Jump in Serious Crime Here Reported by FBI," Capital Times, Sept. 20, 1968

Staff, "Police End Quizzing of Ex-UW MD," Capital Times, Sept. 21, 1968

Staff, "City and County Police Out of UW Murder Case," Capital Times, Oct. 3, 1968

Staff, "Seek Michigan Tie To Slaying At U.W., Similarities Noted,0" Capital Times, April 19, 1969

June Dieckmann, "Co-ed Slaying Tie to Michigan Eyed, UW Chief Plans Comparison," Wisconsin State Journal, April 19, 1969

Staff, "Detectives Check Other Co-ed Deaths," Wisconsin State Journal, April 22, 1969

Staff, "Madison Police Probe Slayings In Michigan," Capital Times, April 24, 1969

Irvin Kreisman, "Chistine's Murder: Still No Clues A Year Later, Police Continue to Work on Mystery," Capital Times, May 26, 1969

Staff, "Officials to Seek Michigan Link to Rothschild Death," Capital Times, Aug. 6, 1969

Staff, "Fager Calls Go-Go Probe Waste of Taxpayer's Money, 'D.A. Should Know Better,'" Capital Times, Feb. 11, 1970

Staff, "Person Quizzed In Campus Death," Capital Times, March 4, 1970

Staff, "Two Years Since Unsolved Murder of Co-ed at U.W." Capital Times, May 26, 1970

June Dieckmann, "Two Years Later, the Hunt for Co-ed's Slayer Goes On," Wisconsin State Journal, May 27, 1970

June Dieckmann, "Murder of Christine Rothschild Still Unsolved After Four Years," Wisconsin State Journal, May 28, 1972

Tom Hibbard, "Portage Stabbing Tie to Rothschild Case Probed," Capital Times, Aug. 25, 1972

Staff, "Link Studied to UW Killing," Wisconsin State Journal, Aug. 26, 1972

Staff, "Stabber of Portage Girl 'Tied' to Rothschild Case," Capital Times, Sept. 16, 1972

Steven Lovejoy, "Rothschild Case Tie-In? New Link Is Eyed to Coed's Slaying," Wisconsin State Journal, Sept. 16, 1972

Bob Mong, "Most Crimes Go Unsolved – Here Too," Capital Times, Nov. 11, 1975

Bob Mong, "Rumor Persists – Madison Is 'Easy' for Criminals," Capital Times, Nov. 11, 1975

Staff, "Police Check Out Possible Rothschild Murder Suspect," Capital Times, Dec. 20, 1975

Staff, "Murder Suspect Investigated for Rothschild Killing," Capital Times, Dec. 24, 1975

Warren Gaskill, "Unsolved slayings – somewhere, someone knows..." Capital Times, Jan. 12, 1978

June Dieckmann, "Police detective whose job was murder retires," Wisconsin State Journal, April 28, 1978

Walt Trott, "Gumshoe's life exciting, but not like Magnum's," Capital Times, Aug. 24, 1984

Sharon D. Pitman, "Chief deputy says goodbye after 28 years," Capital Times, June 11, 1987

Bruce Kauffman, "He's seen it all: protests, murder, trees," Wisconsin State Journal, March 26, 1990

Staff, "Seven murders unsolved," Wisconsin State Journal, April 12, 1994

Doug Moe, "Sister's slaying still haunts her," Capital Times, May 6, 2006

Lisa Schuetz, "Unsolved 1968 Murder: UW woman met violent death," Wisconsin State Journal, May 27, 2006

George Hesselberg, "The 1968 murder at UW still stings, Killer of women has not been found... yet," Wisconsin State Journal, May 4, 2008

Staff, "Memorial to be held in 1968 UW killing," Wisconsin State Journal, May 21, 2008

Steven Elbow, "Lost in the Shuffle, Police have thrown out or lost evidence in at least four Dane County cold cases," Capital Times, Nov. 24, 2010

*The book, "Murder on the 56th Day, Christine Rothschild, First Homicide Victim on UW-Madison Campus," by Linda Schulko was also used extensively as a source.

Chapter 2

Debra Bennett

Floyd Nelson Jr., "Body Identified; Cause of Death Still Unknown," Capital Times, July 24, 1976

June Dieckmann, "Woman found dead in ditch was native of Ridgeway," Wisconsin State Journal, July 24, 1976

Floyd Nelson Jr., "'Big City' Wasn't Answer for Small Town Girl, Police Seek Clues in Death of Debra Bennett," Capital Times, July 24, 1976

Staff, "No new clues in woman's death," Wisconsin State Journal, July 25, 1976

Staff, "Murder Victim Was Last Seen Alive on July 10," Capital Times, July 27, 1976

Staff, "Police ask help in murder case," Wisconsin State Journal, July 28, 1976

Staff, "Murder Victim's Father, 58, Dies," Wisconsin State Journal, July 28, 1976

Staff, "Slain woman, dad have joint funeral," Wisconsin State Journal, July 29, 1976

Staff, "Help sought in murder case," Wisconsin State Journal, Aug. 13, 1976

Staff, wire service reports, "Drifter may be tied to unsolved area murders," Jan. 14, 1984

Associated Press, "Police compare notes on murder suspects," Wisconsin State Journal, Jan. 19, 1984

Staff, Joseph A. Joe Crook obituary, Wisconsin State Journal, Oct. 2, 2007

Debra Jayne "Debbie" Bennett, findagrave.com, May 17, 2011

Chapter 3

Julie Hall

Mike Stamler, "Woman's body identified; police suspect homicide, She may have been sexually assaulted," Capital Times, June 23, 1978

Staff, "Body is identified as library worker," Wisconsin State Journal, June 24, 1978

Staff, "Police ask help in murder," Capital Times, June 24, 1978

Staff, "Still no clues in probable murder," Capital Times, June 26, 1978

Staff, "Crime unit seeks information on dead woman, 19," Capital Times, June 27, 1978

Staff, "Police seek clues in woman's death," Wisconsin State Journal, June 28, 1978

Staff, "No clues in Hall murder," Capital Times, June 29, 1978

Julie Ann Hall obituary, Wisconsin State Journal, July 8, 1978

Staff, "Tests fail to give clue in murder of woman, 19," Wisconsin State Journal, July 13, 1978

George Hesselberg, "Julie Hall's death unsolved a year later," Wisconsin State Journal, June 18, 1979

George Hesselberg, "Four dead, police 'waiting for a break,'" Wisconsin State Journal, May 2, 1981

Staff, "Recent slayings still unsolved," Wisconsin State Journal, March 5, 1982

Marvin Balousek, "Killer to be queried in Texas on state deaths," Wisconsin State Journal, Jan. 27, 1984

Sharon D. Pitman, Mike Miller, "Killer may never face trial here," Capital Times, June 15, 1984

Sharon D. Pitman, "Mass murderer coolly describes area deaths," Capital Times, June 16, 1984

Marvin Balousek, "Evidence 'strong' Lucas killed four women here," Wisconsin State Journal, June 16, 1984

Richard W. Jaeger, "Detective won't soon forget mass killers," Wisconsin State Journal, July 12, 1984

Marvin Balousek, "Accomplice may provide information," Wisconsin State Journal, July 12, 1984

Marvin Balousek, "Killers may represent new breed of murderer," Wisconsin State Journal, June 17, 1984

Marvin Balousek, "Killer's calm shocks local detective," Wisconsin State Journal, June 17, 1984

Staff, "Two state deaths tied to mass killer," Capital Times, Aug. 4, 1984

Associated Press, "Lucas charged in Georgia deaths," Wisconsin State Journal, April 7, 1985

Associated Press, State Journal staff, "Lucas says all but 3 killings are hoaxes," April 14, 1985

Marv Balousek, Kim Schneider, "Madison-area murders in '80s included coroner," Jan. 3, 1990

Dana Brueck, "Murder of Julie Hall," NBC15 News WMTV-Madison, Nov. 17, 2010

Chapter 4

Julie Speerschneider

Staff, "20-year-old woman reported missing," Capital Times, March 31, 1979

Staff, "Missing woman, 20, sought," Wisconsin State Journal, April 1, 1979

Staff, "Search fund started for missing woman," Wisconsin State Journal, May 17, 1979

Bill Jolin, "Couple seeks funds to look for missing daughter," Capital Times, May 17, 1979

Bill Jolin, "Hypnosis 'last resort' for area police," Capital Times, May 18, 1979

Staff, "Benefit to help locate Speerschneider," Wisconsin State Journal, July 27, 1979

Mike Miller, "Body identified as Julie Speerschneider," Capital Times, April 21, 1981

Anita Clark, "Woman's body in Dunn is identified," Wisconsin State Journal, April 21, 1981

Staff, "Cause of death 'undetermined,'" Capital Times, May 7, 1981

Staff, "Victim's sarape," Wisconsin State Journal, May 7, 1981

George Hesselberg, "Retiring city detective leaves with one regret," Wisconsin State Journal, Oct. 9, 1983

Marvin Balousek, "Lawmen return after quizzing killer," Wisconsin State Journal, June 13, 1984

Marvin Balousek, "Mass killer blamed for city murder," Wisconsin State Journal, Aug. 4, 1984

Associated Press, "Convicted killer Lucas visits California; 15 murders solved," Capital Times, Sept. 7, 1984

George Hesselberg, "Pioneering policewoman Mary Ostrander, 60, dies," Wisconsin State Journal, Sept. 21, 1994

Chapter 5
Susan LeMahieu

Staff, "Man charged in threat," Capital Times, Sept. 6, 1979

Staff, "Woman is missing," Wisconsin State Journal, Jan. 25, 1980

Staff, "Body found in Arboretum," Wisconsin State Journal, April 18, 1980

George Hesselberg, "Death of woman found in UW Arboretum called 'suspicious'" Wisconsin State Journal, April 19, 1980

Steven Elbow, "To catch a cold, Investigators admit

to frustration over unsolved murders, but press on to find killers," Capital Times, Sept. 2, 2009

Ruth Ann "Dutt" LeMahieu obituary, Gunderson East Funeral & Cremation Care, Nov. 6, 2013

Chapter 6
Shirley Stewart

Staff, "Middleton girl, 17, missing," Wisconsin State Journal, Feb. 14, 1980

Staff, "Coroner says body is Middleton teen-ager," Capital Times, July 18, 1981

Robert Freimuth, "Body identified as Middleton girl," Wisconsin State Journal, July 18, 1981

Shirley Eileen Stewart obituary, Wisconsin State Journal, July 20, 1981

Staff, "Cause of Stewart's death still unknown," Capital Times, July 21, 1981

Staff, "Death cause not shown by autopsy of girl's body," Wisconsin State Journal, July 22, 1981

Staff, "Notice of hearing, Termination of parental rights," legal notice, Wisconsin State Journal, Aug. 27, 1981

Marvin Balousek, "Detectives have wish list, too," Wisconsin State Journal, Jan. 4, 1982

Euene A. Stewart obituary, Capital Times, May 3, 2002

Chapter 7
Donna Mraz

Sharon D. Pitman, Mike Miller, "UW student murdered on campus, Stabbed behind Camp Randall," Capital Times, July 2, 1982

Dan Allegretti, David Blaska, "Donna: bright, bubbly, unafraid," Capital Times, July 2, 1982

Staff, "Things were 'going great' for Donna," Wisconsin State Journal, July 3, 1982

Staff, "2 more attacks mark outbreak of assaults," Wisconsin State Journal, July 3, 1982

Marvin Balousek, "Few leads in murder," Wisconsin State Journal, July 3, 1982

Sharon D. Pitman, "UW murder stymies police," Capital Times, July 3, 1982

Marvin Balousek, "Few clues, holiday hamper murder probe," July 4, 1982

Associated Press, "Coeds feel vulnerable after attack," Wisconsin State Journal, July 6, 1982

Mike Miller, "Cops appeal for information in slaying," Capital Times, July 6, 1982

Mike Miller, "Man sought for questioning in Mraz slaying," Capital Times, July 7, 1982

Sharon D. Pitman, "In wake of Mraz murder, students feel unsafe on Madison streets," Capital Times, July 8, 1982

Marvin Balousek, "County's top sleuths probe puzzling homicides," Wisconsin State Journal, July 9, 1982

Sharon D. Pitman, "Stained jeans found near murder site," Capital Times, July 9, 1982

Mike Miller, "Lab results coming on jeans found near UW murder site," Capital Times, July 12, 1982

Diane Worzala, letter to the editor, "Worzala lists ways to improve women's safety," Capital Times, July 12, 1982

Sharon D. Pitman, "Analysis of blue jeans in Mraz

murder expected by weekend," Capital Times, July 14, 1982

Sharon D. Pitman, "Jeans not tied to Mraz murder, officials say," Capital Times, July 16, 1982

Marvin Balousek, "Night transportation for women gains," Wisconsin State Journal, July 22, 1982

Mike Stamler, "Solutions to sexual attacks sought," Capital Times, July 27, 1982

Marvin Balousek, "UW murder reward set," Wisconsin State Journal, July 31, 1982

Staff, "Little new in Mraz case," Capital Times, Aug. 4, 1982

Mike Stamler, "Rising rural crime sparks call for volunteer patrols," Capital Times, Aug. 12, 1982

Rob Fixmer, "Cop warns UW women: 'Get street wise,'" Capital Times, Aug. 24, 1982

Mike Stamler, "Late bus service? Costs put damper on idea," Capital Times, Aug. 25, 1982

Marvin Balousek, "Detectives hot, cold on major crime cases," Wisconsin State Journal, Aug. 29, 1982

Staff editorial, "Late ride options," Wisconsin State Journal, Aug. 30, 1982

Staff, "July busy for police," Wisconsin State Journal, Sept. 1, 1982

Victoria McGlothren, "Citizens air views concerning city bus-service alternatives," Sept. 10, 1982

Staff, "Sex assault drop credited to murder probe," Wisconsin State Journal, Sept. 18, 1982

Mike Stamler, "Women may get evening taxi break," Capital Times, Sept. 21, 1982

Staff editorial, "An investment in safety," Capital Times, Sept. 23, 1982

Sharon D. Pitman, Mike Miller, "Woman sought after being stalked near Camp Randall," Capital Times, Oct. 26, 1982

Marvin Balousek, "Police study murder, women-trailing cases," Wisconsin State Journal, Oct. 28, 1982

Marvin Balousek, "Body of murder victim exhumed," Wisconsin State Journal, Nov. 3, 1982

Anita Clark, "Man charged with 3 counts of sex assault," Wisconsin State Journal, Jan. 19, 1983

Patricia Simms, candidate profile, Donald Michelson, Wisconsin State Journal, Feb. 8, 1983

Staff, "Death marred routing 1982 for UW's police," Wisconsin State Journal, March 16, 1983

Marvin Balousek, "Year later, slaying remains a mystery," Wisconsin State Journal, July 1, 1983

Sharon D. Pitman, "Two murders still puzzle," Capital Times, Aug. 25, 1983

Staff, "Reward in Mraz murder case is doubled," Capital Times, Nov. 5, 1983

Marvin Balousek, "$10,000 offered for clue to killing," Wisconsin State Journal, Nov. 5, 1983

Sharon D. Pitman, "Two murders still haunt veteran sheriff's detective," Capital Times, Dec. 13, 1984

Staff, "Milwaukee slaying similar to Mraz case," Wisconsin State Journal, July 11, 1985

Associated Press, "Milwaukee man charged with murder of student," Capital Times, July 12, 1985

Associated Press, "Man, 28, charged in stabbing murder of Marquette co-ed," Wisconsin State Journal, July 12, 1985

Marv Balousek, "Trail cold in unsolved slayings," Wisconsin State Journal, July 9, 1989

David Callender, "10 Years Later, Savage slaying of UW student still unsolved," Capital Times, June 29, 1992

David Callender, "FBI: Killer was would-be rapist," Capital Times, June 29, 1992

Jonnel LiCari, "Crimestoppers now on campus," Wisconsin State Journal, Oct. 6, 1993

Rob Zaleski, "Cop thinks '82 murder will still be solved," Capital Times, June 11, 2004

Letter to the editor, Ned Pondry, "Dane County investigators admit to frustration over unsolved murders, but press on to find killers," Capital Times, Sept. 9, 2009

Ashley Matthews, "Mraz murder investigation," NBC15 News WMTV-Madison, Nov. 2, 2015

Chapter 8

Genetic Testing Solves Wisconsin Cold Case

Ivan Moreno, Associated Press, "Arrest in 1976 cold case stuns Northwoods town, Genetic genealogy used to find match to DNA," Green Bay Press-Gazette, June 5, 2019

Kent Tempus, "Cold case closed: 84-year-old man gets two life sentences for 1976 double homicide in Wisconsin," Green Bay Press-Gazette, Aug. 27, 2021

Chapter 9

Mistakes Lead to Lost Evidence

Steven Elbow, "Lost in the Shuffle, Police have thrown out or lost evidence in at least four Dane County cold cases," Capital Times, Nov. 24, 2010

About the Author

Kevin Damask has worked as a journalist and writer for almost 20 years. His work has been honored with several awards from the Wisconsin Newspaper Association for excellence in journalism. Since 2022, Damask has served as a writer-editor for the U.S. Department of Veterans Affairs, capturing Veterans' stories for the *My Life, My Story* program. He lives with his wife, Jenny, and son, Jackson, in Sun Prairie, Wisconsin.

For more information about *COLD* and to keep up to date on other projects Kevin is working on, please go to Kevin's blog at kevindamask.substack.com.

If you enjoyed reading *COLD*, please leave a review on your favorite book website, such as Amazon and Goodreads. Kevin appreciates the support.

www.ingramcontent.com/pod-product-compliance
Lightning Source LLC
Chambersburg PA
CBHW022049020426
42335CB00012B/617

9781949085907